THE BOW STOPS HERE!

Mary Smale

" ... The lights came up. The conductor and I stepped out onto the stage. The orchestra was huge. The audience was massive. My sister was the concert master. The piano seemed further away than I remembered it. There was a clarity I hadn't experienced during the rehearsals. The piano keys seemed brighter. When I sat down, I could have sworn the keys were swimming back and forth. I prayed, "God help me!" The keys stopped swimming.

The audience waited. On the podium, the conductor paused, and then with one percussive move cued the crash of the orchestra's first chord and my frantic, passionate musical ranting began. "

Cover Artwork by
Lauren Rosales

Copyright 2017
ISBN 978-0-692-36416-1
Smale Publishing

It is with deep gratitude that I acknowledge Dr. Shinichi Suzuki, whose precise written instructions to string students to "stop the bow" became the hallmark of my teaching for decades and has made all the difference in virtually every performance endeavor in life.

— Charl Ann Gastineau

Is this a book about stage fright? And if so, why? Who is going to need it besides performers?

EVERYONE! The world is a stage. Stage fright is a universal problem. You can experience stage fright in any of life's paths: interviewing for a job, teaching a class, addressing the TV camera, speaking to the PTA. or walking out onto an actual stage on which you are the designated performer. Stage fright, or performance anxiety, comes from anxiety which in turn comes from fear. Fear of what? Fear of mistakes -- mistakes from being ill prepared. This book addresses that. And tells you how to fix it. It takes you from the stage fright of the instrumentalist to the martial artist to the teacher in front of the TV camera, to the victim of a robbery, and much much more.

So, pay close attention and have fun on your journey to anxiety-controlled perfection in your life's performances!

— **Mary Smale**

To Bob Smale, my husband and mentor

Table of Contents

Foreword 6

About the Book 8

About the Title 8

About Teaching 9

A Note To My Sister, Mary Smale 9

Introduction 10

About Us 12

A Letter from Eva Masarang 13

Chapter One – The Violin 14

Chapter Two – Piano 44

Chapter Three – Martial Arts 66

Chapter Four – Teaching: Mathematics and Drawing 80

Chapter Five – Science Opinions 90

Chapter Six – Extreme High Anxiety (EHA) 96

Chapter Seven – Drawing Zone 104

Chapter Eight - The Performance Zone 106

Chapter Nine – Letters of Endorsement 110

Conclusion 118

Epilogue 121

Websites 122

Bibliography 123

Acknowledgements 124

Index 126

Foreword

The Bow Stops Here – Not Another Music Instruction Book!

In my humble opinion, having been a singer/songwriter for 50 years and a guitarist for 57 years, performing in numerous band and solo settings, I can say that the music instruction world does not need another theory or speed-building book. Using the wonderful materials already existing helped me to develop my chops and keep my music machine well-oiled. What these materials did not do, however, was prepare me to deal with performance anxiety. Sometimes it struck like lightning just as I was about to launch into a song that required sureness of purpose. It is hard to sing convincingly when you are petrified, or to play movingly when your hands won't stop shaking.

No, to my thinking, what the musical instruction world needs is The Bow Stops Here! It describes a method that eliminates anxiety from the practice sessions before it can strike! Mary Smale, with decades of professional performance to her credit, has applied a brilliant, easy-to-grasp approach to avoiding the contemplation of mistakes. That contemplation of mistakes -- past, present and future -- leads to the anxiety that will spring up from the subconscious at the least opportune times – on stage -- to erode confidence and to rob the performer of the joy of performing.

Mary has tested the Bow Stop method in other areas of performance, one being martial arts, and found the techniques to be solid and sound. I wish I had taken the Stop Bow approach in the 1960s when I was developing my performance-self; it would have made the ensuing years much more enjoyable.

But you, dear reader, can take advantage of this marvelous concept and develop your performance to its full potential. I suggest you introduce Bow Stop into your practice regimen as soon as possible so you can enter a whole new world of musical achievement and enjoyment!

Michael Leppert

From Mary:

About the Book

I've written this book in the dreaded first person singular because it is about all the different ways the Stop Bow Method has impacted *my* life. More precisely, it is about my experiences with Stop Bow (SB) in all the different avenues down which my life has taken me. Due to this, references to me, myself, and I became unavoidable. I hope, however, that some of my experiences line up with at least some of yours so this approach can help spur you towards anxiety-controlled perfection in your pursuits as well.

About the Title

(This explanation is for those of you who may have fallen asleep in your American History class.)

The phrase, *the bow stops here,* is a play on President Harry S. Truman's motto, "The buck stops here." When Truman said, "The buck stops here," he meant that instead of deflecting blame for mistakes, the buck, meaning the blame, stopped at his desk, where he assumed total responsibility. Likewise, the Stop Bow Method requires the violinist to stop and assume responsibility for the next note. The difference being that with the Stop Bow Practice Method no buck will be passed because mistakes are purposely never allowed to occur.

From Charl Ann Gastineau:

About Teaching

There is a kaleidoscope of approaches to teaching a student to play an instrument. I use the Suzuki Method for a myriad of reasons, and to it I've added my Stop Bow Method to further reduce mistake-driven anxieties. I'm constantly adding to my curriculum, especially when I find something that works well for another teacher. We all learn from each other, and should always be open to new ideas.

A Note To My Sister, Mary Smale,

Thank you for the many hours you have spent reading, writing, re-writing, asking endless questions, using the method, and all the other exploratory work you've done over the past years that have enabled you to write this book.

Thank you for using this method in so many areas of your life thus showing the wonderful benefits of the Stop Bow Method in both the music and non-music world.

Thank you for showing that this is a comfortable way to learn and a comfortable way to teach because it eliminates the many hours of correcting mistakes which lead to frustration for both student and teacher.

The Stop Bow Method has served me well for twenty-five years, and I know it will smooth the path to success for everyone.

Charl Ann Gastineau

Introduction

Charl Ann Gastineau has often said: "Who wouldn't want to learn a piece of music perfectly in a few weeks rather than badly in a year?"

There are teachers, and there are innovators, and then there are innovative teachers. My sister, Charl Ann, is one of the latter. She has taught hundreds of violin students over the years and has raised their performance levels to heights that few of them even thought possible. She did it by introducing some of the most innovative educational practices in the profession. I've brought some of these to light in this book, and one of them is the major focus of the book – the one Charl Ann calls Stop Bow (we call it SB for short). The Stop Bow Method is a unique practice method that centers on perfect practice sessions. The method contains controversial aspects that not only make it unique but make it work. In these practice sessions no mistakes are allowed to occur. With the absence of mistakes goes the anxiety that the contemplation of mistakes causes. So the practitioner isn't practicing anxiety while he's practicing the music.

"Why," you may ask, "am I writing about my sister's violin teaching methods?" I'm doing this because I believe that when someone has developed something that offers so much promise to others, it should be widely shared.

At the age of five, Charl Ann picked up the violin and never really put it down. It has been and continues to be an important part of her life. Her college major was music. She attended several universities because her violin performances took her from Los Angeles to Las Vegas, and finally all the way to Honolulu, where she performed at the Top of the Ilikai Hotel for two years while completing her degree at the University of Hawaii. There, her journey took another turn when she met a young design engineer, Donald Gastineau, who worked at a facility on Johnston Island and flew to Honolulu on his days off. On one visit, he just happened to see Charl Ann performing at the Ilikai. From that point on, his destination for his days off was the Ilikai. After much planning, they both decided to change their career directions so they could be together. She decided to move back home to California and teach violin. Soon after she left, Don resigned his post on Johnston Island and flew to California as well, where their wedding took place. Eventually, he took a job as a design engineer at Litton Industries and Charl Ann began teaching at the University of Southern California (USC) Preparatory School of Music in Los Angeles, which is now known as the Colburn School. She taught there for eleven years. It was there that she was introduced to and began employing the Suzuki Method. She was so impressed by the method that she enthusiastically joined the Suzuki Music Association of California (SMAC). This association with the Suzuki Method and SMAC would continue for the next forty-two years. Later, she and Don moved to Camarillo, in Ventura County, where she began teaching privately. It was here that she developed and honed her innovative practices.

So, this is indeed a book about the wonderful method that my sister, Charl Ann Gastineau, has developed for teaching students to play the violin. But it also explores how this valuable method can be applied far beyond violin instruction. We'll see how her singular strategy, Stop Bow, can be applied to many disciplines, from the mastery of a musical instrument to a visual art form, a classroom subject, or even an athletic pursuit. When combined with the student's dedication, it can result in the perfection of that skill.

Gastineau's Stop Bow Method teaches students how to be fully focused, fully consumed, and how to become one with their endeavor. Other teachers have alluded to a slowed-down learning process, but not to the degree that Charl Ann has taken it. She answers the questions: *When, Where,* and *Why* do we stop the bow, and ***what is happening during the stop?*** Most teachers simply teach what they have been taught, but it is the innovative teacher who *builds* on what she's learned and refines it for the generations to come. It is the innovative teacher who, in daring to chart another course, is willing to weather criticism and controversy to push her students to the highest level of mastery they can achieve.

I used my sister's method in the practice of both piano and martial arts. Later on, I found the method impacting my teaching of mathematics and art. I even employed it in my preparations for my math teaching shows on the TV program, Homework Hotline. In this book, I've shown how the Stop Bow Method wove its way into each of my disciplines and literally changed my life. Her method effectively levels the playing field so anxiety-controlled perfection is attainable for all students willing to diligently follow her path.

So, this isn't a book about how to play an instrument or move in martial arts, rather it's a book on a method of practice that leads to an anxiety-controlled perfection in performance.

About Us

To better understand the perspective from which this book is written, you should know that I am a pianist, a martial artist, and a middle school math teacher.

I've been playing piano since the age of four and for the first 23 years, piano was my life. In college I majored in music, with an emphasis on piano. I taught piano. Piano defined me. I even married a renowned jazz pianist and music arranger, Bob Smale.

Then I discovered the martial arts. To date, I've earned black belts in four different styles of martial arts: Tang Soo Do (first degree), Tae Kwon Do (first and second degree), Hapkido (first, second, and third degree), and Aikido (first degree), and I have won black belt *kata* divisions of local, national, and international competitions and was rated in the 1990s. I studied martial arts for nearly twenty-five years, and taught them for thirty.

Math is another of my passions. It became my college minor. I taught middle school and high school mathematics for more than thirty years. For almost three years, I taught algebra and geometry on a local television show, *Homework Hotline* on KLCS-TV, Los Angeles.

My sister, Charl Ann, is an accomplished violinist. She's performed with a number of musical groups including The Acousticats, Phil Salazar and Friends, and has worked with a number of orchestras. Some of the albums in which her violin is prominently featured are: *The Time Between*, by Kate Price, (I heartily recommend the selection, "Tango of the Flowers" which can be heard on YouTube); Radio Rails, by Jackie Pierce and Dave Borough; and The Cat's Meow by The Acousticats, (check out "In Memory of Elizabeth Reed," which can be heard if you Google "Phil Salazar's All Time Favorites."

But in this book we will focus on her accomplishments as an innovative teacher. Here she has augmented her students' musical knowledge by expanding her music program to include other instruments (including the mandolin and other stringed instruments) and styles (one of which is bluegrass) and her Stop Bow Method , which has produced phenomenal results.

Testimonial letters from Charl Ann's students have been included in the final pages of this book. These letters describe how the Stop Bow method not only brought perfection to their performances, but benefited other areas of their lives as well. The letter from Eva Masarang, however, is included here at the beginning because she is not a student, but the mother of a student, and her letter hightlights the attitude of students and parents who are new to the Stop Bow Method – a "Do I have to do it this way?" attitude that prevails until they finally discover that the method actually works.

A Letter from Eva Masarang

For the past four years, my now fourth-grader has been learning to play the violin using his teacher's Stop Bow Method; however, it is only fairly recently that we truly began to appreciate the method. Learning an instrument requires daily practice and that requires a significant investment of time. It is the quality of practice, however, that dictates the end results, and this is where the Stop Bow Method has truly become invaluable for us. Using the Stop Bow Method ensures that the time spent practicing is quality time which ultimately results in beautiful music.

Initially in my son's violin journey, each practice session involved me. I learned the music so I could help him. Pretty quickly he surpassed my capacity to learn and teach. So I switched to paying careful attention to the music and to watching him meticulously to check for mistakes. Having absolutely no musical background, this was immensely difficult and required constant vigilance on my part.

Well, this past summer my son practiced the same songs faithfully every day, but without necessarily using the Stop Bow Method on every occasion and without my constant supervision. In the fall, when it came time to select songs for the upcoming recital, it turned out he had not mastered the songs he had practiced all summer and was not able to play them at a recital. While initially surprised, given the months he had spent practicing the music, I realized I needed to be more involved. However, given that I was truly unable to keep up with the music, I felt lost.

When I asked my son's teacher, Charl Ann Gastineau, for direction, she reiterated the Stop Bow Method and its benefits. I started having my son pay careful attention to each note and each detail. He played slowly and carefully, stopping his bow on each note as he named the note and its bow direction. He did this for the next two months but we still had doubts. My son had not played the music once from memory and we both were unsure if he could. Our instructions were to just use the Stop Bow Method while looking at the music, and we followed our instructions faithfully. To be honest, both my son and I were fairly certain he could not have mastered the music since he had never tested his ability to play it from memory. Well, we were both in for a shock, because when he played the music for our teacher the week before the recital, he played it beautifully, from memory.

As an adult, I can see how well the Stop Bow Method worked. However, what really speaks volumes about the method is that my son is now a believer. In the past, getting him to use the Stop Bow Method was often a struggle. He would resist, especially once he felt he knew the piece. But now, when he is either practicing a performance piece, or learning a new piece, he willingly does the Stop Bow Method. He does so because he knows the Stop Bow Method provides beautiful results.

Chapter One – The Violin

The Suzuki Method

The Suzuki Method didn't just slip quietly into music teaching curriculums around the world. No, it exploded upon the scene. World wide acclaim was given to Dr. Shinichi Suzuki when tiny children hardly more than toddlers were skipping that awkward squeaking squawking stage that is so characteristic of early violin playing, and going directly to *actually* playing music. The level of proficiency of the Japanese students that toured with Dr. Suzuki when he brought his method to the world was unmatched. Teachers everywhere were flocking to the method. It was like cool water in the desert. He was offering an instructional method that opened up the possibility of excellence in violin performance to virtually all students. Eventually teachers of other instruments saw that the method could be adapted for their students as well. Dr. Suzuki died in 1998 at age 99, but his movement is still growing and many of the artists on today's concert stages were students trained in his method.

One of the primary reasons for this explosion of interest is that the Suzuki Method provides for the training of the entire body: it employs the muscles, the senses, and the soul. But it starts with the ear. So, before ever approaching the music, the student has become familiar with it because he has heard it from several sources including recordings, concerts, and recitals. Immersion is the key. Because of this immersion approach, the student is able to begin playing the instrument immediately, without the insistence that he be able to *read* the music before playing it.

Dr. Suzuki's method uses the mother tongue approach. Just as a child learns his spoken language by being immersed in it – hearing it and then speaking it daily — he learns the language of music by hearing and then practicing it daily. Dr. Suzuki pointed out that a child learns even the most intricate aspects of language from his mother, father or another caregiver with no problem. Immersion and repetition are the keys, and no pedantic learning has to take place for this to happen. Simply being present is all that's required. Note that a child doesn't have to know how *to read* the words he speaks in order to speak them. Likewise in the Suzuki Method, a child doesn't have to know how to read the notes he plays or sings in order to replicate them. Theoretically, however, with this immersion method, a child's ear can become so proficient that he may try to circumvent reading music all together, but teachers who employ the Suzuki Method are prepared for that. They find ways to creatively slip reading music into their curriculum for those reluctant students. Charl Ann makes reading music a part of her Stop Bow Method, so it slips seamlessly into her lessons from the very beginning.

When discussing the Suzuki Method, Charl Ann reminds us that Mozart and Beethoven honed their musical talents by first being immersed in music. These men were born into musical families. So, one could say that music was the *other language* in their homes. Parents teach language, be it words or music, by example in the presence of their children. Since children are, by their very nature, learning sponges, they soak up any language to which they are continuously exposed, whether it be their family's spoken language or music. Centuries later, Dr. Suzuki advocated that the parent be the real violin teacher. This would necessitate, however, that a parent learn to play the violin, so he or she would be able to communicate in the language of music with the child.

Erosion in the Digital Age

When I reflect upon our childhood, I cannot remember a time when music wasn't a part of our home life. It seems our parents instinctively knew we should be surrounded by music. Nowadays, however, the pressing demands of the digital age take precedence over things like that. Time or the lack thereof is the problem, and even the *idea* of family members gathered around a piano seems quaint, and likely unattainable. Most parents are simply spread too thin to take a major role in their children's education. In a perfect world, the Suzuki Method of immersion by a parent surely works, but the twenty-first century has not produced that perfect world.

Even though most teachers know the positive impact that parental participation can have on a child's musical education, some have been forced to accommodate the parents' time constraints by allowing the parent participation to be reduced to simply being present at the student's lesson. In other words, the teachers were faced with a dilemma: either reduce the parent's anxiety level by reducing their level of required participation, or risk their students having to quit music. Now the teacher must become creative to make up for the reduced parent participation. How can this be accomplished? By following Dr. Suzuki's lead to keep the music exciting, interesting, and fun.

Keeping the Interest

Dr. Suzuki stressed that students should have fun during lessons to inspire them to press on through tougher times. He knew that any training only becomes effective with the cooperation of the student. In other words, when a student's interest wanes, learning often stops. It has to be fun, and part of the fun is creating something interesting, like beautiful music. Even back in the early nineteenth century, Chopin created *etudes* to train students' fingers to perform intricate moves. But these *etudes* are not just exercises, they are also beautiful pieces of music. Wise teachers have always known it is important to capture and retain students' attention by infusing their training with fine music. Dr. Suzuki does it with the carefully chosen music in his method books. Charl Ann now does it with a combination of the Suzuki Method's predominately classical repertoire, fiddling, and mandolin. But, as with any successful method, her program had to evolve.

Evolution of the Program: Who Is the Teacher Here?

Like any other teacher, Charl Ann has had to weather the challenge of teaching uncommitted, uninspired students over the years. She constantly searched for tools to cure these conditions. She eventually found that she was reinventing her method for each student. She says she is convinced that *her students are teaching her* as she teaches them. She believes it is an ongoing reciprocation. Since each student is unique, by listening she learns what approach will best meet each of their needs. She believes that all students come with some kind of gift, so the teacher serves her student best when lessons are formulated around that gift, while expanding their musical knowledge. For example, if the student has developed a pitch memory, Charl Ann knows that this student may find his notes with more ease than a student without such a memory. The pace of the lessons may move along faster with such a student, as it might for a student who has greater enthusiasm for the instrument, or one who is by nature a hard worker, or one who has a greater ability to focus, or those who desperately want to please their parents. These are positive gifts. But, what happens when we can't find such a gift? Just persevere, because it might be hiding. A case in point: recently Charl Ann had an experience with one of her students that illustrates how a teacher can learn from a student. In this case, the student's gift was being overshadowed by what appeared to be a handicap.

To set the stage: This student is a child who has difficulty naming a note before she plays it. Charl Ann, as part of her Stop Bow Method, requires the beginning student to speak the name of the note and the bowing direction before playing each note. This activity has multiple benefits the greatest being that it ensures the student maintains focus throughout the practice.

Because of her difficulty doing this, the child was beginning to develop a negative attitude. Her mother noticed this at the lesson, so she set about searching for a solution to the problem. The next week she came bubbling into the lesson, excited about what she had discovered during her daughter's week of practice. First, the mother was aware of the child's gift – the ability to sing. So, since the student liked and was good at singing, the mother asked her to put the violin down and simply sing the names of the notes — all Suzuki students know the music in their head from exposure to it. She then asked her to pick up the violin and say only the bowing directions during the *stop* before playing each note. Then, when the activity went back to saying the name of the note and bowing direction before playing, it was noticeably better, and so was the student's attitude. So they successfully backed into the activity through the student's gift – a student teaching her parent and her teacher.

The renowned violinist Itzhak Perlman said, in a recent interview on the Tavis Smiley Show, that *"when you teach others, you teach yourself."*

From meager beginnings, Charl Ann's program grew to more than 60 private students a week. How did this happen? What caused the explosion of interest?

Charl Ann credits several major changes: her insistence on perfection through the Stop Bow, two mandatory lessons a week (the second being a workshop), learning an additional instrument (mandolin), active parent participation, additional styles of music (bluegrass, folk, and ethnic), the addition of fiddling, and incorporating good ideas gleaned from her fellow teachers.

A Favorite Idea from another Teacher

Charl Ann isn't above borrowing good ideas from her fellow teachers. Here is one of her favorites.

Among music teachers, the general consensus is that the more times the student performs before an audience, the easier it becomes. Recently, Charl Ann learned a technique for lessening performance anxiety from a neighboring piano teacher, Julie Elliott. Julie had found a way of getting the students to play multiple times during the course of each recital. This is what she does. First, she has renamed her recitals *Piano Parties*. In the spirit of this party, she has the students start performing as they arrive – completely informally – *before* the recital begins. Since the students don't all arrive at the same time, some students are playing as the audience arrives. This way, no time is lost. The first student to arrive will likely play his first piece only for the teacher and his parents. The audience grows as the other students arrive. After each student has played one of his seven performance-pieces (all students have seven recital pieces ready at all times), they make the rounds again, playing a different one of these pieces. In this casual atmosphere with people milling around finding their seats, they go around four or five more times before the recital actually begins. By that time each student has already performed multiple times — some of them have played as many as six of their recital pieces. Now, when the program actually begins, each student has lowered his anxiety level in this atmosphere of camaraderie, and raised his confidence level as well. And, she has found that heightened confidence may well carry over not only into subsequent performances, but into other avenues of the students' lives as well. In her piano parties Julie Elliott has found a way to maximize the students' benefits from each recital.

Fiddling

The online encyclopedia, Wikipedia, says that the difference between the classical violin and fiddling styles is in the *degree* in which the style is impacted by ethnic or folk music traditions. Fiddling is a violin-playing style that has roots all over the world. Wikipedia lists fiddling styles from Europe, the Americas, Africa, Australia, Cape Verde, and India. Each country puts its cultural imprint on fiddling. In the U.S., among the myriad of styles that have evolved here, the most well known of the *traditional* styles is bluegrass, which comes to us from Appalachia. This bluegrass, in turn, has its roots in Irish, Scottish, Welsh, and English traditional music, crossing the Atlantic with immigrants. Later, African-American influences were included through jazz. With the incorporation of jazz, the bluegrass style stepped from the traditional into the modern realm and is now listed among modern styles as well. Charl Ann chooses an eclectic program with a combination of ethnic tunes and bluegrass.

The fiddling in her program beckons the student in because it's fun, exciting, and interesting. It causes everyone – participant and listener alike – to smile. It has broadened the students' horizons and has become a wonderful adjunct to the traditional classical music of the Suzuki Method. Charl Ann uses the fiddling lessons to further develop each student's ear and creativity. She begins by teaching him short fiddle tunes (two lines, sixteen measures) by demonstration – one measure at a time. The student then duplicates the music by ear (hearing it then playing it). The more he plays by ear, the better he will be at locating the notes on his instrument. Then he is instructed to practice the tune at home with the sheet music. Here, before the adoption of the Stop Bow Method, the student was simply instructed to practice with the music. Now, however, he is to practice the piece using the Stop Bow path on both violin and mandolin with the music. Eventually he is instructed to begin practice without the sheet music. Without the sheet music, the piece will begin to change. When this happens, the improvisation door begins to open.

How the Fiddling Began
Besides teaching, Charl Ann has always performed with established musical groups. In the 1980's she was a member of the Ventura County Symphony Orchestra which was under the direction of Frank Salazar. It was here that she met the conductor's son, Phil Salazar. Phil, aside from being an accomplished violinist, is also a renowned fiddler. When he invited Charl Ann to one of his "gigs," she was so impressed by his amazing technique, the music's rhythms and the excitement it evoked — the way Phil made his violin almost *talk* to the audience — and the fact that a person couldn't stay sad listening to his music, that she decided to incorporate it into her teaching program.

She then discovered that fiddling comes with another perk: local, state, and national *fiddle contests*. Charl Ann began encouraging her students to enter these contests and some of them became so dedicated to the music and so adept at playing it, they began winning these contests. Now her students experienced being exposed to different types of audiences: the critically appreciative classical music audiences and the enthusiastically passionate fiddle music audiences some of which could number in the thousands.

She also introduced them to a wonderfully supportive organization called The California State Old Time Fiddlers Association with its District 8 branch in Oak View, California. The organization exists to preserve and perpetuate the old time fiddle style. It provides an opportunity for fiddlers to get together twice a month for fiddle performances, and to join in jam sessions. Once a year, District 8 hosts the Southern California Regional Fiddle Contest. So the organization effectively takes on the job of keeping the excitement going in the interim between these regional and the national fiddle contests.

In another effort to maintain the enthusiasm, the District 8 chapter also publishes a bi-monthly newsletter. In it they sometimes include inspiring letters from their readership. It was in one of these news-letters that a child wrote of the positive impact fiddling can have on a family when she related how fiddling had united her family. They had eventually formed a family band and hit the road to compete in contests all over the Western United States. The hardships they en-countered on the road: getting stranded — out of gas and money and having to do some street performing to make enough gas money to get home; getting caught unprepared in subzero weather and having to sleep all huddled together in their car to survive the night so they could compete in a contest the next day, tightened the bond they had as a family. She concluded by expounding on how these and other experiences molded and strengthened their family, and how their ex-tended family of fiddlers from the association had not only kindled their enthusiasm, but had provided them with the wherewithal to keep going and succeed through adversity.

Armed with the enthusiasm fiddling evokes, Charl Ann eventually joined Phil Salazar's bluegrass band, The Acousticats. Now, with two fiddlers, the band's style expanded to include twin-fiddle music, and in 1982 Phil and Charl Ann became the California State Old Time Fid-dlers Association twin-fiddle champions. It was an exciting time and the group became very popular. Their albums began getting more air time on the radio. They even had a tune on the country music charts, "Hey, Hey Evangelina," written by one of their former members, Cyrus Clark. The group is still performing to enthusiastic audiences under the names, Phil Salazar and Kin, or Phil Salazar and Friends. Even with all this outside activity, my sister's teaching program kept expanding.

Other Avenues to Success: All Charl Ann's Violin Students Play Mandolin.

Another prominent instrument in bluegrass music is the mandolin. Strung like a violin but with frets and double strings, the mandolin uses the same fingering as the violin but it is plucked, so there is no need for a bow and it is held and played like a guitar. When she put a mandolin into her students' hands, they were amazed that they could already play simple tunes. There was an instant affinity. The students were excited by the intrinsically beautiful tone of the mandolin, and the fact that they were immediately *successful* in playing it. So it met one of the criteria for promoting learning – it met the need for the student to experience success.

Eventually, the student is introduced to chords so he will be able to begin thinking vertically while accompanying soloists on fiddle tunes in the workshop.

The Workshops: The Magic
Charl Ann required parents to commit to two lessons a week, the second being a workshop. During workshops students had the opportunity to hear each other play, to solo on both violin and mandolin and to accompany the fiddle tunes on mandolin. Some parents attending the weekly workshop became interested in studying guitar so they could participate in the workshop. They became so proficient on their guitars that they eventually were able to accompany their children in the fiddle contests.

Parent participation has from the beginning been monumentally important in the Suzuki program. Student success is often directly proportional to the participation of a parent. With the fiddling, some of Charl Ann's students' parents became so involved that they would drive their child to contests all over the state and sometimes even out of state. Their enthusiasm spread to their children who in turn began winning the contests. Five of these families even formed family bands and toured the country: The Giacopuzzi family named their bluegrass band *Pleasant Valley*. Other families that formed bands were the Francom family that played Irish Music, the Ron Fink family that played Klezmer music, the Sharma family that played music from India, and the Rivera family that named their band Mariachi Camarillo. Eventually, some of the students branched off to form their own working musical groups. Two of them are Ashley Broder and Kimmy Francom Dubois, who have toured the U.S. and Europe with their respective bluegrass groups. Some of the others are Lauren Donahue, Adam Giacopuzzi, Jimmy Kappen, and Sameer Sharma. All of these successes were a direct result of those weekly workshops.

Mandolin Success Stories
Some of the students became so proficient on the mandolin that Charl Ann in 1997 petitioned to allow a group of them to perform at

the Southern California Junior Bach Festival, Ventura County Branch. It was something that had never been done before, since the Bach Festival had long been a venue for performances on traditional classical instruments such as piano, violin, and cello. In spite of that, the group was given the green light to perform.

Five handsome young men carrying beautiful mandolins presented a striking picture on the stage that day and the fact that their performance was outstanding only added to their impact. They performed the third movement of Bach's Third Brandenburg Concerto. They concluded to enthusiastic applause. Afterwards each of the judges made a point of congratulating Charl Ann on having the foresight to broaden her students' musical education by playing traditional music on a non-traditional instrument. It should be noted here that the mandolin, though not currently considered traditional in classical music is, in fact, a very old instrument. Vivaldi, Mozart, and Bach all wrote music for the mandolin in the eighteenth century.

Within the year the same group, this time in tuxedos, performed the same selection at the Thousand Oaks Center for Performing Arts in Thousand Oaks, California, before a packed house.

Here is an interesting aside: the lead mandolinist, Keith Giacopuzzi, had for years simply attended his brother's weekly violin lessons and sat in the next room doing his homework. His only connection to the music was in hearing it week after week –immersion. Then one day he decided to get involved. This speaks volumes for success by being continuously exposed to the music, because even though Keith had never played an instrument before, and didn't read music, he learned the mandolin and led the mandolin group at the Bach Festival. Several months later he further amazed everyone when he soloed to a packed house with the New West Symphony at the Thousand Oaks Performing Arts Center on a Vivaldi Concerto written for mandolin.

At the time, he was a high school student and a member of the football team. The night of the concert, the whole team came and sat in the front row of the concert hall to watch their teammate perform.

The orchestra, made up of adult professional musicians, was seated on stage awaiting the appearance of the soloist — Keith. Then the tall, slender 14-year-old stepped out onto the stage and took his place on a podium in front of the orchestra. He looked cool, calm, and collected as the orchestra began the introduction. The house waited with bated breath to see if this young man would be able to weather the stress of this situation. And then — he began to play, with the most beautiful, clear, professional technique imaginable. In the words of his father, "He nailed it!"

It was astounding that a young man who never played a musical instrument before studying the mandolin could hold an audience of classical music lovers spellbound with his performance of a classical work — on a mandolin. But he did.

Imagine the tears of pride from his parents, teacher, teammates, siblings and me. He concluded to thunderous applause. In 2000, he was named Discovery Artist for the New West Symphony. This experience let him know he could do anything. Nothing scares him now.

The Lament

In spite of all the positive changes, the excitement and the expanded participation, there were still problems. The biggest complaint — the lament of all teachers – was having to *continually correct mistakes.*

The following was my sister's description of her job as a music teacher.

"After twenty years of teaching violin, I found that 90 percent of my time was spent correcting mistakes, and the other 10 percent was spent telling the students to slow down. I found that my frustration came from an annoyance with myself: I had not found a way to teach the students to avoid these mistakes. And, I realized that my *telling* the students to slow down wasn't a solution to the problem of recurring mistakes, because by the time I was telling them to slow down, it was too late; they had already solidified the mistakes in their muscles and that created an anxiety that would be exacerbated during any future performance of that piece.

Someone once said that anything you've ever experienced is *in your brain* and, in our case, your muscles as well – forever. With the proper stimulus *it will surface.* The students were experiencing this *cycle of mistakes and corrections* over and over again, so it was no wonder they kept making them."

It was then that Charl Ann began to seriously tackle the problem that would ultimately result in her Stop Bow Method. She began by first developing two lists: The Nine Potential Mistakes in Violin Technique and, The Ten Fundamental Elements of Aggravation.

The Nine Potential Mistakes in Violin Technique:
1) Poor intonation
2) Poor tone
3) No dynamics
4) Not making clean string changes
5) Incorrect bowing
6) Rhythm problems
7) Wrong fingering
8) Poor form (position/posture)
9) Slow shifts

The Ten Fundamental Elements of Aggravation:
1) Learning a piece of music unevenly;
2) Procrastination, which often stems from a fear of failing;
3) Worry that today's practice won't be as good as yesterday's;
4) Running out of energy after ten minutes, which happens when beginning a practice session by playing the music at full speed;
5) Never feeling comfortable with the entire piece of music;
6) The first page of a piece is always played better than the rest of the piece;
7) Dynamics are not always heard because the differences between loud and soft become blurred;
8) Bow not straight and/or wrist not flexible;
9) After-vacation worries about getting back into the routine;
10) Sight-reading problems.

There were clearly so many things that could go wrong that would eventually have to be corrected that Charl Ann began asking herself what could possibly be done to break the cycle of mistakes and corrections. Having decided that training on an instrument could be approached in the same way some Olympic athletes train, with hours of slow practice, (even professional runners' first moves are slow) Charl Ann surmised that students may do more to create correct muscle memory and staying power if they practice *super slowly*. However, she realized that no matter how slowly you play you are still running out of bow, and trying to think about creating perfection while the bow was still moving was creating unwanted anxiety. She finally decided that "slow" wasn't good enough. She would have to go to "stop."

So, she again stepped out of the box and directed her students to go from slow practice to "stop-the-bow practice." The stop comes *before* rather than *after* the note is played. During that interval of seeming inactivity, the student is contemplating what is required to make the playing of the upcoming note perfect. So if you do all your preparations while the bow is stopped rather than while the bow is still moving, you'll avoid the anxiety that comes with contemplating your next note while you're still playing the note that came before.

The Origin of the Stop Bow Method

Now I come to the crown jewel of my sister's method of teaching violin, the means by which she and her students can avoid all mistakes: the Stop Bow Method. This is the key to learning a piece of music perfectly from the first time it's played. Charl Ann no longer has to correct mistakes because with the Stop Bow Method, there simply aren't any.

Charl Ann has always believed that music teachers, no matter how accomplished they are, need to continue their own music education with a master teacher. In the '80s she was studying with her master teacher and she was, of course, experiencing the universal frustrations of all students: that same cycle of mistakes and corrections. It has been said that the definition of insanity is doing the same thing over and over and expecting a different result. So she decided she needed to do something *different*. She reflected on what every teacher says after every mistake: "*Slow down.*" She analyzed the situation and asked herself, "How slow should slow be?" And then, "Should slow for the sake of slow be all there is? Shouldn't the slow be more productive than that? Shouldn't there be something going on during the slow to positively impact the music?"

As an experiment, Charl Ann decided to slow to a complete *stop* before playing each note, to actively contemplate that note, to ensure perfection in every possible way: posture, position, energy, intonation, fingering, bowing, dynamics, rhythm, etc. She would then play that note perfectly, observing every aspect of a focused performance. Then she stopped the bow again and prepared to execute the next note *perfectly.* After this initial trial, she took a fresh piece of moderately difficult music just two pages long, and experimented with it. She meticulously stopped the bow before playing each note, to make sure each note she played would be perfect. It took her forty-five minutes to complete the piece in this way, but she was excited because, although it was slow, she had achieved *perfection playing a brand new piece.* She had no anxiety or regrets. Regrets come from reflecting on mistakes, and there were none! Best of all, she wasn't tired. After forty-five minutes of work, instead of being fatigued, she was actually energized. She could hardly wait for the next day's practice session.

For six straight days she did *exactly* the same thing, but on the seventh day it became impossible to maintain the same deliberate, stop-and-go speed. She felt an overwhelming need to increase the tempo. But she only allowed herself a very slight increase in speed. In other words, she would *only play at a speed that would ensure perfection.* She knew it would still be perfect with only that tiny increase in speed. She continued in this way, increasing the tempo by tiny increments every few days throughout the month, always being careful to *play only at a speed that would ensure perfection.* She deliberately decided to refrain from playing the piece at full speed until she got to her lesson with her master teacher.

Arriving at her lesson, she had no concerns at all. Her confidence level was at its peak (one of the perks of this method of practice). Halfway through the first page, playing at full speed, the teacher yelled, "Stop!" It shocked her. But he then clarified: *"Heifetz couldn't have done it better. What did you do?"*

This was a defining moment for her. She now had a tool to change the cycle of mistakes and corrections that had always plagued students. Stopping the bow had forced her to take more time *initially* to save time *ultimately.* In other words, students would be paying it *up front* during those long Stop Bow sessions so they wouldn't have to pay it *forever* by correcting mistakes. Charl Ann remarked, "Of course, who wouldn't want to learn a piece of music perfectly in a few weeks rather than badly in a year?"

Thinking back to that day, what was it Charl Ann's teacher heard in her performance that caused him to ask, "What did you do?"

He knew she was a good violinist when she first came to him for lessons months before. What was it he heard in her delivery that day that was different? Well if you'll recall, one of the comments Charl Ann made when she arrived at her lesson that day was that she *had no concerns.* This was an affirmation that she was not only about to take the stage but to own it. It was a level of confidence her teacher had not seen or heard before. SB had delivered the final component: *Confidence.*

Was it difficult to get students to stop the bow? Oh, yes. It was like trying to hold tightly to the reins of an excited horse because the student knows the music in his mind and soul before he ever plays a note. He has absorbed the music through listening to excellent recordings by great artists, or he has listened to more advanced students perform it at numerous recitals. It was no mean feat to keep the students' fingers from running ahead of their brains. So, to guarantee a student uses the method, she takes them through it at the lesson and their parents are asked to continue this instruction at home. She may even instruct the student *not* to practice the new piece at home, to keep him from practicing it without Stop Bow. He will then play it only in her company for the first few weeks. The week without practice is not lost time because this is seasoning time for the muscles. And this seasoning is occurring on a perfect start to the music. She says that in the lesson, she watches the student's fingers so she can stop the student before the finger goes down wrong — to avoid the mistake. She likens the mistake to a wound. Even after the wound heals, it leaves a scar. The scar is a reminder of the wound. Charl Ann says that if the student has already made the mistake, trying to correct it is like trying to erase the scar. Practice makes perfect is a saying we've all heard. But practice does *not* make perfect unless the *practice is perfect* – every aspect of it.

The following, which is a narrative from Charl Ann, may be confusing, but read through it anyway. You'll see the attention to detail that is needed as the student focuses on every aspect of the performance. And you'll find that this level of focus could be applied to any discipline.

Charl Ann's Narrative and Her Steps for a Stop Bow Practice:
With the Suzuki Method, the student has heard the music multiple times before he starts to learn it. So his mind already knows it. Now, using the Stop Bow practice method, he will connect his mind to his muscles (focus) so anxiety-controlled perfection will be achieved when this new piece reaches performance level.

Note: Since it is important to begin each practice session with Stop Bow, begin with your *newest piece* because it is already in the initial stages of Stop Bow. If, however, time dictates that you limit the practice exclusively to your performance piece, then begin the practice with Stop Bow on that performance piece, and repeat the piece with connected bows at a moderately slow tempo. For each repetition maintain the focus and increase the speed until it is at full speed.

1) Check your complete form – feet, both left- and right-hand positions, shoulder, and chin.

2) Check the bowing direction (up bow or down bow) of each note.

3) Position the bow on the string at the appropriate place: frog, middle, or tip.

4) Carefully center the bow between bridge and fingerboard with the hair slightly tilted toward you.

5) Observe the key signature and beginning dynamics. Beginning students must name all notes and bowings aloud. For example: "C-sharp, down" or for two slurred notes, "C-sharp, E, down, down."

6) Check the first note for intonation, making a very tiny sound. Every note in the piece is quietly checked before the power stroke. Such checks should continue during each successive practice so that by the time the piece is at performance level, the intonation is perfect, *without* constant checks. If the piece hasn't been performed for an extended period of time, resume those checks during practices prior to a performance.

7) For a loud note (*ff*), Dr Suzuki says play with a power stroke speed bow. In other words, a slight tug on the string and then a speed power stroke without pressure – using only the weight of the bow.

8) For a soft note (*pp*), use a tiny powered stroke which begins with a tug on the string by the bow and a quick release of the pressure.

9) For double stops, check each note of the double stop separately, and then play the two notes together slightly louder, to ensure the interval is perfectly in tune. Then play them with the full stop bow.

10) Observe the rhythm mentally. Since all the notes (strokes) are of the same duration, the wait time between notes determines the rhythm. In other words, the rhythm is observed by simply allowing a longer wait time for longer notes.

11) Hold your position and continue to maintain it through the above eleven-step preparation for the next note.

Note to teachers: students may tend to relax (rest) once they've performed the note perfectly. Perhaps they feel they are entitled to rest after being successful with that one note. Don't allow it.

If the violin student is doing all these things, he reins in all the scatterings of his conscious mind and directs his muscles to one focal point – the note. And this total muscle-connected focus allows *no mistakes*. With Stop Bow there are no easy or difficult passages. They are all of the same degree of difficulty. The student should never underestimate the positive impact on his muscle memory of playing a note perfectly with total brain and muscle connection, even just once.

The next day's practice continues from exactly where the student left off the day before, so no part of the piece is played more often than any other. This means the student should *not* go back to the beginning of the piece until he has played it through to the end.

As already stated, it is of paramount importance that you begin each practice with Stop Bow. "Why?" you may ask. Because, besides concentrating your focus and training your muscles, it gives you the *energy* that will sustain you throughout the entire practice session. As you begin to increase your speeds you will be playing with slow connected bows instead of Stop Bows, but the focus the SB evokes is still active. Remember, *you can only play at a speed that ensures perfection.*

The SB that each new piece begins with and the eventual focused connected bows can also effectively eliminate the dreaded plateaus.

Plateaus May Disappear with SB

The plateau is the level the student reaches where he remains for extended periods of time, without progressing. With SB, the student is always progressing, albeit slowly. If the students remember to begin each practice with Stop Bow and to maintain that high level of focus throughout the practice, their subsequent performances will be perfect and in line with their level of achievement.

Seasoning Time

Seasoning time is built into the early SB practice sessions by the rule that the student is only allowed to play the piece once a day. Then, he steps away from it until tomorrow. The time away from the practice is almost as important as the time with it. It is the *seasoning time*. Your muscles are resting comfortably with their new knowledge. Allow them this time.

Students find it difficult to resist the urge to play the new piece more than once a day. Perhaps they are so excited with their new-found method that yields perfection that they are impatient and don't want to wait until tomorrow to play the piece again. They may feel they are wasting time. If the student gives in to this urge to repeat the new piece multiple times today, his focus may start to suffer, and this leads to mistakes.

Subsequent SB Practice Sessions

Contemplation, preparation, and checks will eventually become automatic, and will take less time. *Stop* and *slow* are built into the system, but the more you do it, the faster the prep time and checks between notes will go. So for the younger or beginning students, the prep time will be longer than that of the advanced students.

The First Experience Using Stop Bow with a Student

Soon after I discovered the Stop Bow Method, one of my third-year students asked me if she could learn a fiddle tune she had recently heard an advanced student perform. She wanted to play it in a contest that was coming up in just three weeks. I told her she needed to pick a piece that was less difficult, one that could be comfortably prepared in that amount of time. I could see she was disappointed, so I decided to tell her about the Stop Bow Method. She was so pleased that there was a way she could get the piece up to performance level in three weeks that she listened intently to the steps she would need to follow in her upcoming practice sessions. Since she was so completely motivated, I knew the method would work for her.

Lesson One's Practice Steps:

1) Name all of the following out loud:
    a) The key signature
    b) All the sharps and flats in that key, in order
    c) The time signature and explain it
    d) The first note and bow direction
    e) If the note is "slurred" (connected to its neighbor), say the name of both notes and then say the bow direction. For instance "B-flat, C, up, up (or down, down)
2) Assume a good position.
3) Check every note to be played for intonation *before it is played* by playing a tiny bow, just loud enough for you to hear. For double stops, check each note separately and then check them together. This will ensure that when each note is played, it will be perfect.
4) Check dynamics. If the dynamic is loud (*f*), play the single note with a full bow. If it is soft (*p*), play the single note with a tiny stroke. If you are slurring two or more notes, divide the bow stroke accordingly.
5) Play each note with a power stroke and speed bow, always with beautiful tone. All bows must be stopped and open-ended (the bow permits a continuous ringing sound even though it has stopped and remains on the string).
6) Your brain already knows the piece of music from multiple listening sessions. That means it knows the rhythms as well as the melodies

and harmonies, so you are teaching your muscles what's required of them spatially during the stop. You are to take all the time you need to complete the note you are on perfectly. The rhythm is in your head at this point. When the practice progresses to slow connected bows, the rhythm will be more recognizable.

I told her to follow this procedure for every note in the piece *each day*, and she was to play the piece completely through *one time only each day – repeating nothing and making no mistakes.*

Lesson Two:

When she came to the lesson the following week, she assured me she had followed my instructions exactly and she demonstrated it for four measures by stopping before each note was played and preparing for it by naming the note and its bowing direction and then playing that note perfectly and with beautiful tone. I could see she had practiced correctly. The next step was to name only the bowings before playing each note. When she did this correctly, I had her name only the notes. After a few more successful bars of the piece, I had her continue the Stop Bow, this time without saying anything out loud. Everything was observed perfectly. To be sure nothing would change during her second week of practice, I asked her to practice at home just as she had the previous week.

Lesson Three:

When she came to the lesson after the second week of practice, I had her suspend all vocalization, and the two weeks of SB had allowed her fingers to become so comfortable with the notes that she was able to play the piece perfectly at a moderate tempo. I didn't have to correct anything. Now she could practice the piece multiple times every day using the music and moving from SB to slow connected bows to slight speed increases in those connected bows until she finally reached performance speed. The student was so successful that I then knew the process would work for all my students.

Offering Stop Bow to the Rest of the Students

This was my first experience seeing a student succeed with the Stop Bow Method. I then began introducing my most motivated students to the SB. They began attaining levels that far exceeded expectations. When these students performed before other students at the workshops, the students who were listening came to realize that if they wished to attain those levels of perfection too, Stop Bow was the way to get there. Now this practice method could be implemented by *all* my students.

Before the Performance

You may be asking, "When do the repetitions, so necessary for performance, enter into the practice sessions?" Since all performance pieces are *old* pieces that have already had numerous repetitions, and lots of seasoning time, the student will now only need to begin a fifteen-day regimen of repetition (fifteen times a day for the fifteen days prior to the performance) to be completely ready for performance. Toward this goal, I implemented what I call my 15/15 chart. The chart holds a 15-day countdown to the performance date. The student then marks on the chart the number of times he actually plays the piece each day. The goal is 15 times, but that doesn't always happen. To lessen the monotony of all these repetitions, I have a required regimen for the practice. These repetitions will be broken up to include:

1) Two times perfectly, with SB, observing the rhythm — the SB at the beginning of the 15/15 practice ensures the energy and focus for the fifteen repetitions will be maintained;
2) Four times perfectly, with slow, focused, connected bows, observing the rhythm;
3) Six times perfectly, increasing the speed each time the piece is repeated with focused connected bows, but slower than the performance speed;
4) Twice perfectly, playing it with the recording the teacher has made with the metronome clicks audible in the background;
5) Once perfectly, playing at performance speed.

Back to Mary's Narrative

I inquired about the rehearsal recording the teacher makes with the metronome. Charl Ann said that most performances increase in speed once the performer steps in front of an audience. She requires the student to play along with the recording's slow metronome-driven pace to ensure he won't slip into the runaway speed the performance-generated adrenaline is likely to produce. She adds that even before the 15/15 sessions begin, the student has been practicing with this recording.

I also inquired about using the metronome from the beginning to ensure the rhythm is followed. Charl Ann reiterated, "Don't forget that the student already knows the music, including the rhythm, in his head because of all the listening he's done." His first job now is to teach the music to his muscles. She added that the metronome's relentless beat pushes the student to the next note whether his muscles are ready or not. The initial Stop Bows are designed to train the muscles to memorize the spatial requirements of the note. If the student is concentrating on getting to the next note on time instead of focusing on the total preparation for that note, he will create anxiety that will likely continue to accompany that note every time he plays it. So, he won't use the metronome because it doesn't beat slowly enough.

The Secret's Out

As I said earlier, other teachers have emphasized the need for students to practice slowly, but none, to my knowledge, have advocated practice that is so slow that it stops before each note is played to allow the student to focus and connect the brain and the muscles to ensure the execution of that note will be perfect. I, however, know of a musician whose practice, though not quite stop bow, was close to it.

One summer, through the efforts of my teacher, Ethel Bartlett, I received a scholarship to the Santa Barbara Music Academy of the West in Montecito, California. This is a very prestigious academy. The draw for students is that each student gets the opportunity to study with renowned artists. I was privileged to study with Gyorgy Sandor and Emanuel Bay. The academy staged an opera, complete with orchestra, at the end of the summer session. The opera was performed for the public. There were three performances at the Lobero Theater in Santa Barbara.

Because I had to pay for my own room and board, and since I couldn't afford the dormitory, I elected to stay at a co-op with three other students — two rather hefty opera singers and a tiny violinist, all of us in our early twenties. The little house had two bedrooms, so the singers took the larger room, and the musicians, the violinist, Louise and I, took the other.

Occasionally, Louise would practice her violin in our bedroom. I could only describe the music Louise was creating at these practice sessions as *painful*. The music – if one could call it that – was unrecognizable. There were no melodious sounds emanating from that room. I found myself wondering how she got into the academy if she couldn't play any better than that. I knew, however, that Louise was a remarkable sight reader. She could read even the most difficult music on piano as well as violin. Musician lingo for a highly-proficient sight reader is: "She can read *flyspecks*." She was a genius. But her practice sessions on violin left a great deal to be desired.

One day, Louise knocked on my practice room door to invite me to her master class performance. I found myself feeling sorry for her because of the music I had heard her play, but I said, "Sure." Then I asked her what she would be playing. She said she would be playing the first movement of Symphonie Espagnole, by Edouard Lalo. I was shocked because this is a very difficult work, and if the musician is not up to it, it becomes immediately evident within the first notes played. I was hoping the shock wasn't registering on my face.

I arrived at the concert hall at the appointed time. The master class waited while Louise took the stage. The pianist played the introduction. I steeled myself against what I believed to be a moment of shame for Louise — and then Louise lifted her violin to her shoulder and with a huge display of confidence she *attacked the music and took over the stage.*

At this point my eyes widened and my jaw dropped. I couldn't believe those sonorous, robust tones were coming out of little Louise's violin. She fooled us all. Her outstanding talent had been kept a secret. But now the secret was out. In retrospect, I believe Louise had discovered a method that rewarded her with success: A method that may very well have been like a precursor to Stop Bow. All her practices had been slow, quiet, unrecognizable, focused, private affairs. She didn't care to entertain herself or anyone else. She was there for the job of learning.

An Interesting Aside

I spoke recently to a musician friend of ours, Bob Reynolds, a chemist by profession. He began to reminisce about his first encounter with Charl Ann's method. When she first described it to him, he began to wonder if her Stop Bow Method would work on piano. He recalled that he had listened intently to her instructions and had even written them down. Immediately upon returning home, he began applying it to his piano. First he pulled out a Beethoven sonata he wasn't familiar with. He stopped and checked the key signature and, because he wasn't familiar with the piece, scanned the first measure to establish the rhythm in his head. Then he checked all the aspects of the first note (a chord), named all the notes in the chord and placed his fingers over them. When he felt he was ready to play the chord perfectly, he did. Naming all the notes in the chord aloud forced his focus to remain strong throughout his practice session, and the stop allowed sufficient time for his muscles to *feel* the notes. He continued through the sonata doing the same thing for each note. If he felt his focus waning, he stopped and marked where he had stopped. The next day, he started where he had left off. So, no part of the music was played more than any other part. Because every note or chord was played independently and perfectly, he had no mistakes to correct. There were no passages in the music that were difficult when the notes were played this slowly. No anxiety wove its way into the practice because there were no mistakes or difficult passages.

He did this for several weeks. He practiced as though he had all the time in the world. This allowed for the seasoning time for his muscles and his brain. Then he began increasing the speed, but only slightly, *to allow only a speed that would ensure perfection. Each practice left him feeling energetic and excited about the next day's practice.*

Finally, when the piece reached performance level, he had achieved a level of perfection that amazed him. He began performing the number whenever the opportunity presented itself — until he was well into his eighties. This approach allowed him to feel confident in his performance, knowing he would *own the stage.*

Viewing a SB Success

I recently attended Charl Ann's spring recital. I was a few minutes late, so as I approached the entrance of the church where the recital was already in progress, I heard the strains of a concert violinist floating from the entrance. I wondered who that could be.

On stage was a young woman who was clearly a working concert violinist — she played with that professional degree of energy, confidence, and perfection. There was also the crispness of attack, and the definition of each note that are the hallmarks of a professional. The church was filled with Charl Ann's students who all sat transfixed.

As I watched, I smiled because here was the final stage, the one the students were striving for. Here in front of them, they were experiencing live, the essence of the Stop Bow Method.

The young woman, Rebecca Kappen Tseitlin, came at Charl Ann's urging to kick off the recital. She was a former student of Charl Ann's who took her SB practices very seriously and became a concert violinist. And here she was — living breathing proof of what the students could achieve using the method. They could actually hear the SB in her performance. It gave it an all-encompassing definition. Because of the standard she was setting for the recital students – who all now sat at rapt attention – they would surely push themselves to even greater heights. And they did.

In Summary

The frustration that teachers experience from repeatedly correcting their students' mistakes, reached its apex in the early 1970s for violinist Charl Ann Gastineau, driving her to seek a different path. Instead of repeating the words "slow down" and "focus" over and over, she decided to have her students slow down to the point where they actually *stopped the bow*. Then she taught them how to achieve the mind-to-muscle focus that would fit into that lull during the *stop* before each note was played. With this approach to every note, no anxiety was being perpetuated and the mistake-correction cycle stopped. The Stop Bow Method is designed to eliminate anxiety from practice sessions, which in turn allows the performer to be in control of any anxiety that may crop up during subsequent performances.

The controversial elements that make the method unique are also what make the method work. These elements include:

1) Only allowing perfection to occur on every note, no matter how long it takes to achieve it. This way, anxiety from the contemplation of mistakes doesn't creep into the practice. In other words, the student won't be practicing anxiety right along with the music.

2) Only allowing the piece to be played once during each practice session because playing a *new* piece multiple times during a single practice session will lead to a waning of the focus. One perfect focused practice is better than multiple imperfect ones. Save the repetitive practices for performance pieces. Then, repeat each performance piece fifteen times per day for the fifteen days prior to the performance.

3) Only viewing and practicing the new piece as a unit. That means no part of the piece will be played more than any other part. If the piece cannot be completed in one practice session, mark the spot where the stop occurred and resume from that spot at the next practice.

4) No passage in the piece is to be viewed as being more difficult than any other, and it won't be when played one focused note at a time.

It soon became evident that this method could be applied to other disciplines beyond the practice of violin. It levels the playing field so that perfection in performance is available to whoever stays on the SB path regardless of the platform.

Q & A (Charl Ann answers the most frequently asked SB questions)

Pitch (Intonation)
Q: How does the violin student ensure correct pitch during SB practice sessions?

A: Checking, checking, and more checking. Quiet checks always occur before the actual note is played. Some ways of checking are playing tiny scales up to the note, or checking the fourth finger note against the neighboring open string.

Before I discovered the SB practice, I'd start my practice sessions by simply reading through the new piece. Of course it would be riddled with mistakes, but I found that 90 percent of the mistakes had to do with intonation. And I was fixing them *after* they had occurred instead of *before*. With SB, I now check before I play the note to ensure it will be perfect with every practice session.

Amount of Time Using SB:
Q: How long should it take to get a new piece to performance level using SB?

A: The initial SB stage can last a week or more depending on the length of the piece. The slow connected bows with their gradual increases in speed will take as long as it takes. And finally, the 15/15 stage is self explanatory. Putting the added pressure of a time limit on the student will simply lead to more anxiety. However, I issue a challenge to my advanced students as a culminating activity. The challenge is to learn an advanced piece of music in a limited amount of time. I do this to ensure the students use the SB practice method to learn the piece. I am literally setting up one anxiety-provoking situation – the time limit — to keep another anxiety-provoking situation – the mistake-correction cycle — from occurring. They are to learn the third movement of Bach's Violin Concerto in A Minor perfectly in six weeks. This means the piece *has* to be learned using the SB method, because it has to be learned perfectly in less than four weeks. This leaves no time for the mistake-correction cycle to occur, and it leaves the last fifteen days for the 15/15 practice or some other adequate repetition practice regimen.

Even Practice:

Q: Why is it so important to keep the practice *even* in my SB practice sessions?

A: If you take the difficult passages out of the context of the piece to give them more time, you've acknowledged their difficulty which immediately opens the door to anxiety. With SB practice, there is no passage that's more difficult than any other, because each note is played independently and perfectly. If you practice unevenly, that means some passages were practiced more than some others. The passages you slighted will more than likely be the ones that will cause problems during your performance. Remember, it's a head game as well as a muscle-training game. In SB, you learn the piece of music as a unit.

Rhythm

Q: How concerned should I be with the rhythm in my initial SB practices?

A: You will be acknowledging the rhythm by simply increasing the wait time after the longer notes. (The whole note gets more wait time than the half note).

Remember, there is no metronome ticking because that will only introduce another doorway through which anxiety may enter. There is no anxiety because you aren't producing music yet; you are just producing beautiful sounds: you are simply preparing your muscles to recognize the signal from your brain so they can respond appropriately to produce the sounds contained in the music. It's only later, after you have suspended your verbalizations (aloud or silent), and have begun to increase your speed, that the piece begins to become recognizable.

Playing by Ear

Q: Is it good to play by ear?

A: Playing by ear is always good. It allows you to become familiar and comfortable with the instrument. It lets the student be in command of knowing where a particular tone is located on the instrument in relation to the other tones. This allows the student to be confident that he can play any tone he wants at any time he wants, and it will come out just the way he hears it in his head.

Automatic Playing

Q: To what extent should our playing be automatic?

A: One hundred percent. With SB, the music was focused when it went into your muscles, so it will be focused when it comes out in your performance. In other words, on some level the performer's brain is still engaged in that "automatic" performance.

When to Use SB Practice

Q: When should we use SB?

A: Whenever anxiety- controlled perfection is necessary, as it is in performance.

Mistake in SB Practice

Q: I know there are no mistakes in the SB practice, so what happens if there *is* one?

A: If there is a mistake, that means your focus has waned. Stop, and go back later after you have rested and are ready to focus. Don't stress out over the *no mistake* caveat of SB. *SB doesn't mean you can't make a mistake, it means you won't.* Above all, the practice has to be anxiety-free. Relax, take your time: it's easy, it's fun, and it's just practice. Smile, feel, and touch. There is no calendar, no clock. If after seven days, you don't experience that tiny magnetic pull that says *I can go faster now without mistakes*, then do it the same way for another seven days, or thirty days, — whatever it takes.

Fixing a Mistake

Q: What if a mistake has woven itself into the fabric of the music?

A: Then you have no choice; you have to correct this mistake with SB. Often, and especially during the practices just prior to a performance, the urge to cut loose and go faster is so overpowering in a student that he or she stops looking at the music and abandons the SB practice. Just at a time when the SB practice is so critical, the student simply plays his performance piece at performance speed over and over again instead of beginning the practice session with SB. When he does this, mistakes creep into the practice. In order to correct them, I schedule extra lessons so I can supervise the SB practice. First I have the student read the music and SB the faulty passage over and over again, *occasionally* playing the passage slowly with *connected* bows. Then gradually, throughout the hour, working the passage slowly back into the music using both stopped and connected bows. This whole process will be repeated for each lesson. It could take two weeks or more for the mistake to be corrected, but the anxiety the mistake created may possibly remain.

SB and Relaxation

Q: I'm always nervous whenever I play my instrument, whether or not anyone else is listening. Is that normal?

A: It may be normal, but it's not desirable. Make the music the point of the practice. The nervousness means you are setting up an *audience scenario* in your head. Stop it. "How?" you may ask.

Make your practice follow the SB path by redirecting your focus to the contemplation of each note before you play it. If you are busy stating the names of the notes, and the direction of the bow, you won't have time to conjure up an audience.

I always ask my students, "What is the *most important note* in the piece?" After they name every note on the page, I reveal the answer to be, *"The note you are about to play."*

During your practice sessions, keep the music, not the performance as your goal.

Matching the Size of the Violin to the Student

Q: What size violin should a student play?

A: Make sure the instrument fits the student. Consult the violin instructor before purchasing the violin because it's paramount that the student be as comfortable as possible so muscles develop gradually.

Adjusting the Mandolin

Q: Do Mandolins come in different sizes?

A: No. But the mandolin needs to be adjusted to accommodate some students, to keep from stressing the muscles in the hands and fingers. I take each mandolin to a mandolin specialist who puts on soft-gage strings and lowers them so they are close to the frets. This accommodation will make the instrument easier to play and allow the student to develop his hand and finger muscles gradually.

Parent Participation

Q: How long should a parent actively participate in a student's lessons, watching and taking notes?

A: Until the student exhibits the ability to practice correctly without the parent's help.

Performance Pieces

Q: Which of your pieces should go into your list of performance pieces?

A: Old pieces. To clarify, *old piece* doesn't mean a piece from the archive that you haven't played for years. In the Suzuki Method, there is no archive of forgotten music because all the music from the first piece in Volume One to the most current piece being learned by the student is to be kept current because all the music in Dr. Suzuki's method books was handpicked by him to teach specific techniques needed to be a proficient violinist. So, all these techniques have to be practiced. That doesn't mean that at every practice the student is to play everything he's ever known — time constraints wouldn't allow that. It might take several days or weeks for the student to cover everything doing a few pieces at every practice. Since my students learn every piece in the Suzuki books using SB, every piece has gone through the initial SB steps, through the progressively faster speeds of the connected bows, through the 15/15 repetition practices, and finally through the recital so every piece is a potential candidate for the current list of performance pieces.

Why Only Once a Day?

Q: Why do you insist that students play each *new* piece only once a day?

A: One reason is the time constraint. SB practice takes a long time in its initial stages: a two-page piece may take as much as forty-five minutes to get through just once. Another reason is purely psychological: if the student knows he won't have the opportunity to repeat anything today, he will stay focused so he can do it right the first time. And finally, playing the piece more than once a day may lead to increasing the speed too soon, which may cause focus to wane, which causes mistakes to occur, which causes anxiety.

Memorizing the music

Q: Do I have to memorize the music?

A: Often, the need to memorize music causes a pervasive anxiety. If the student doesn't dwell on memorizing as the ultimate aim, the memorizing will occur naturally. (See *A Letter from* Eva Masarang.) I tell my students to always *practice with the music.* I don't use the word *memorize* during the learning process because, once I do, students are tempted to try playing the music from memory too soon.

When to Start/Stop SB?

Q: When should the SB start and stop?

A: The SB begins the first time the bow is placed on the strings and the essence of the SB should continue throughout your musical practices. Simply put, SB is a method of practice that levels the playing field between the student and the music. If the question is: when you reach a high level, can you stop the verbalizations? The answer is that verbalizations can be silent, but the focus that these verbalizations evoke needs to be kept intact. The artist has found his path to success which has included a finely tuned focus. How he developed it we'll never know, but the music student can continue to attain his high levels of performance if he continues along the path of the anxiety-free, muscle-connected focus of the SB.

In One Day?

Q: Can I work up a new piece — from the SB stage, through the connected bows on to performance level – in one day?

A: Yes. As long as you remain focused at all levels. But beware of the pitfalls. Playing the piece multiple times in one practice session will too often cause focus to wane, and mistakes to slip into the practice. And since the student is playing the piece multiple times, he'll begin to stop to correct those mistakes. Now he's into the mistake-correction cycle and the anxiety that goes along with it. The seasoning time that allows the piece to comfortably reside in your muscles is gone. If you really need to do this, I suggest you experiment — pick a short easy piece — see what it will take for you to maintain your focus and perfection through all the stages of the SB practice in one day.

Back Stage – Getting Ready to Go On

Q: Should I play the piece up to speed *just before* I go on stage?

A: No. If you have the opportunity to do any playing of the piece just prior to stepping on the stage, make it a quiet calming SB session. Remember, part of your performance depends on your state of mind, and that last calming SB practice can give you the mind-set for perfection, energy, and confidence. Every practice should begin with SB, but in the case of the performance, the final practice should be SB as well.

Tell Me Again

Q: Tell me again, what I can expect my performance to be when I use SB religiously?

A: Ultimately the performance will be *on purpose* instead of accidental. Confidence will drive the performance. It will have focused crispness of attack, definition, perfection, passion, and boundless energy.

Chapter Two – Piano

Ethel Bartlett Robertson's *Singing Tone* Method: Stop Bow for the Piano

I don't know what drew me to the concert that afternoon. Perhaps it was the frustration and subsequent desperation I was feeling about my piano performances. Perhaps I was ready for a drastic change in my approach — definitely something had to change because I had hit the wall.

The concert hall was small but elegant. Two people – the Robertsons – sat at their respective Baldwin concert grand pianos in the hush before the performance begins. The audience waited expectantly. I don't know what I was expecting — certainly not what I got. Music students see a lot of concerts so we pretty much know what we are about to hear. But I wasn't prepared for the Robertsons.

I was eighteen and eighteen-year-olds don't cry, and certainly they don't cry over a classical piano concert. But soon, there I was with tears streaming down my face. I didn't know you could get that level of passion out of a piano. After all, they were striking keys with their fingers. There are not that many ways to do it. Apparently I was wrong because the Robertsons had found another way.

After the concert ended, Ethel conducted a master class. In it she introduced her secret weapon – The Singing Tone. And, as if that weren't enough, to top it off, Ethel presented one of her students – a fifteen-year-old girl who had only been playing piano three years. Now it was one thing to hear a concert pianist play with anxiety-free perfection, but it's another to hear that level of performance from a student particularly one who'd only been studying the instrument for three years.

Now they had my undivided attention. I knew I needed to study with this woman. I also knew finances would be a deterrent. My wonderful, supportive, but poor parents couldn't handle the added expense of me studying with this acclaimed pianist and teacher. So Ethel took pity on me and allowed me to study with her under a partial scholarship. For me, it marked the beginning of a new era in my quest for perfection.

A Shameful Beginning

While I felt I was a pretty good pianist, I knew my playing could only be characterized as somewhat *frantic*. I suppose I had "passion" and "frantic" mixed up, because almost immediately, Ethel, in her broken English, managed to communicate to me that "frantic" does not allow the audience to relax and become comfortable with your performance.

"Frantic" means you have taken the stage but – *you don't own it; it owns you.*

Much to my chagrin, she started my instruction back at a level that I considered a *pre-beginner.* She simply felt she couldn't begin to build my technique on the holes in my education, and in the very first lesson she introduced me to her Singing Tone Method, which I now realize is very much Stop Bow for piano.

Her belief was that when you perform music, you are actually singing. Singers sing with their voices. Some instrumentalists sing through their fingers. Brass and woodwind players sing through their fingers, lips, and breath. But the artist incorporates his whole body into his performance. Ethel maintained that the fingers were just what made contact with the instrument, but that the music comes from another place inside you and simply flows out through your fingers. Ethel's Singing Tone Method resulted in music so beautiful that it was as though she were able to reach inside the piano and caress the strings to make them sing. As a matter of fact, if you were standing near Ethel while she was performing, you could hear her actually singing – softly, badly, but singing nonetheless. She was so totally focused that she became *one with the piano.*

This is how she made those singing tones happen.

The Singing Tone Touch – Total Focus

Other pianists have made reference to the term "Singing Tone" but Ethel's Singing Tone pulled the student's focus to the surface of the piano key and kept it there. This focus was so strong that it positively impacted every aspect of performance from stage fright to perfection. Here are the initial steps to her Singing Tone Method:

1) Stop, place your finger on the key, and then allow your brain to connect to the tip or pad of your finger. You'll know when this has happened because you will actually *feel* your finger making contact with the surface of the key.

2) Relax and press the key as you would a doorbell: The slight pressure you use for this comes, not from your finger, but from your core and travels up through your arm pit and on out through your finger. The light, doorbell-press of your focused finger causes the strings inside the piano to sing. You will do this for every note you play. This way you are playing each note as though you mean it. In order for me to accomplish this, it took more than a minute to produce just one note. But if I was going to train my body to *work in tandem with my brain, this*

is what it would take. From that day on, I wasn't allowed to play any notes any other way. Initially it took a great deal of time, but ultimately it cut my practice time in half, because it virtually eliminated wasted time — by eliminating mistakes.

The Doorbell Experiment

In order to get the true sensation of the doorbell touch, the student should do this experiment: go to your doorbell and focus on that button which, when pressed, would cause a bell inside the house to ring. Then place your finger on it. Watch what is happening with your body as you press on the button. Even though the pressure is slight, you'll notice that you aren't just depending on your finger to produce the power for that pressure. Instead, the power is coming from your inner core and travels up to the armpit and finally on out through your finger. That focused, anxiety-free touch causes you to actually *feel* the surface of the button and that feeling connects you to the button. Your touch isn't forced, it's relaxed, and you are anxiety-free because the doorbell is *your* doorbell and you know everything about it.

Now, imagine that same touch on a piano key, that same focused, anxiety-free feel. Now imagine doing this for every note you play from now on.

A New Language

It was like learning a new language, the language of this new piece of music. First, you immerse yourself in the language by hearing it over and over; Suzuki students first listen multiple times to the music they are about to learn. Then you read, observing everything about the note you are about to play. As with SB, you may even choose to say out loud the things you observed because vocalizing wakes you up and pulls your focus into the next step which is playing the note with the Singing Tone perfectly. Then when finished, you sleep on what you've heard and said and played — this is your seasoning time. Then you repeat this anxiety-free routine the next day hearing, saying, playing and sleeping — and again the next day, and the next. Gradually verbalizations will be silenced but the focus they evoked will remain, and speeds will begin to increase. Finally, after several weeks of doing this, you will be shocked when one day you find yourself actually conversing (expressing yourself) in the new *language*.

This analogy between the learning of the music language and the spoken language was made clear when I examined it in the light of what happened to a college friend, Gary Davis. Although he wasn't a musician, and the situation wasn't a music scenario, it does provide an interesting parallel. When Gary joined the Navy after finishing college and after "aceing" his entrance exam, he was required to learn Japanese in six weeks.

Each day he sat with headphones on for hours at a time, listening to Japanese. He was immersed in the language, hearing, saying, sleeping, day after day. He didn't believe he was capable of learning Japanese in six weeks. I remember him expressing doubts as late as the fifth week. Then one day, before the end of the sixth week, the phone rang and an excited voice shouted, "I'm speaking Japanese!"

The Similarities and Differences in ST and SB

Ethel's Singing Tone (ST) is the Stop Bow (SB) for piano because the methods do basically the same thing for their respective instrumentalist: creating anxiety-free perfection in the student's practice sessions through enhanced focus. And they follow similar paths in that endeavor: They both *stop* to allow sufficient time for the student to bring his mind to the point on his muscle that makes contact with the key or string that puts sound to the note. The methods are different only because the instruments are different. The pianist, instead of stopping a bow to train his focus in on the next note, will be stopping his finger. Instead of addressing two unconnected tools (bow and violin), he'll be addressing eighty-eight keys and an infinite number of combinations of them. And instead of playing one note at a time, he'll be playing multiple notes of various durations. And since the brain can only concentrate on one thing at a time, he may tweak the SB practices to include *hands-separate* practice. In both cases, however, the thread that connects the two methods is the anxiety-controlled connection of mind and muscles to attain perfection from the soul in performance.

A combination of the two methods could prove beneficial for the piano student.

The idea of keeping and holding focus by stopping to verbalize information about the note is uniquely SB, but addressing each note independently is present in both methods. When using ideas that issue from both methods, the acronym, ST/SB, will be used.

Steps for the ST/SB/Suzuki Practice Session

Since the ST method does for the pianist what SB does for the violinist – connecting the brain to the muscles for perfection without anxiety

— some of the steps look similar. But the violin is a lyrical instrument and the violinist is usually playing one note at a time, and his greatest concern is the creation of the beautiful tone that goes with that note. The piano, on the other hand, is a percussive instrument. The pianist doesn't have to create the sounds that come out of the piano because they are already there. There is a huge harp inside the piano and little hammers that strike the strings of the harp. Together, they create the beautiful sounds for him. He does, however have to strike a key to make it happen. And herein lies his opportunity for expression because his connection to each key must come from his core. So, if you are a piano student on the ST/SB path to anxiety-controlled perfection, you should:

1. As in the Suzuki Method, listen to and digest the piece first before starting to practice it; this way, your brain knows the music before you teach it to your muscles.

2. Begin your practice with your newest piece because it is likely the one that will take the most time (SB).

3. Follow the SB/ST path on this new piece by first observing the key signature, dynamic markings, phrasing, position, and time signature. If you are a beginner, name all these things aloud. Even if you're not a beginner, it may help to keep you awake and focused if you name all these things as well.

4. Write the fingerings for each note, based on where the note occurs in the passage, where it's going, and how comfortable it feels under your hand. You may have to place your fingers lightly over the keys to make that determination. Each finger is numbered (the thumb is one, index finger is two, then comes three, four, and five in order). Writing down the fingerings has multiple benefits: (a) it forces you to *stop* and take the time needed to draw the brain's focus into that finger; (b) it likewise provides the time needed to draw the sensation of playing the *note* into the muscles' memory; (c) it forces you to use the same fingering every time; and (d) it provides an opportunity to work hands separately.

5. Be cautious. In more advanced music the first note is usually not alone. It may be accompanied by another note or notes (forming chords). So prepare each note in the chord so it is under your fingers, ready to be played. Check to see that every aspect of the chord or note is ready: the fingering, duration, touch (staccato, legato, slur), dynamics (loud, soft), and keep the focus. Observe which notes will be released when the next note is played and which notes must be held into the playing of the next note. Now say the name of the note and finger num-

ber aloud or silently, and then play the first note or chord, observing all of the above with the Singing Tone touch — *feeling* the key or keys, pressing it as you would a doorbell. Do not repeat this note or chord today. It was perfect. But continue to hold the appropriate notes through the preparation for the next note or chord (ST/SB).

6. After repeating all the above steps for the preparation of the second note or chord, play it with the ST touch. Continue this pattern throughout the piece. Note: Here you are busy developing perfect spatial patterns in your muscles. You will be taking as much time as you need with your preparations for the perfect execution of each note. Because of this, anyone listening to your practice should not be able to identify what you are playing. Your brain knows the music, so now you are teaching it to your muscles. The process is super slow.

7. Keep repeating all the steps for each note. If you don't finish playing the piece today, mark where you stopped, and pick it up at that spot in tomorrow's practice session. This way, no part of the piece is played more than any other part (SB).

8. These strong focused steps are so slow that time constraints dictate that you'll only play the piece once a day or if the piece is long, once every two days or three days. Don't repeat anything because there is no need, everything was perfect at that extremely slow pace (SB).

9. Sleep on it – this is your seasoning time.

10. Repeat the same routine tomorrow, and the next day, and the next, and the next at the same speed. Eventually, your muscles will let you know they are ready for an increase in speed: the magnetic pull to increase your speed will be overwhelming. When you feel that burning need to increase the speed, do so, but only slightly so you continue to be *present* for every note. *Only accept a speed that will ensure perfection.* By this time the piece will begin to be recognizable to the casual listener. Which means the rhythm is now more discernable because the muscles no longer need long pauses for preparation. Every few days you'll again feel the need to increase the speed. Do it, but again, *only at a pace that will ensure perfection.* This is the pattern you will maintain until you reach performance level (ST/SB).

11. Finally, continue to look at the music when you're practicing, and avoid only half-seeing it: focused reading (SB).

12. Follow the SB path which dictates there are no passages that are more difficult than any other passages. All parts of the piece are of the same degree of difficulty because every note is addressed separately with full focus. Nothing has to be corrected because there were no

mistakes. Relax and smile.

Experiment with ST/SB Practice: Pick a Piece

The aim here is to work a piece up to performance level without creating any anxiety along the way. First, choose a piece of music that won't create anxiety the minute you look at it; nothing in five flats or sharps, or thirty-two notes per measure.

If you haven't played for a number of years, forget about what you were capable of when you last performed. If you were an advanced student, pick something of only moderate difficulty. And make it short, one page or less.

Warning: If you are a halfway decent reader, you'll find it difficult to keep from slipping into sight-reading mode, or if you've learned the music in your head from multiple listening sessions, you may find yourself using your ear to circumvent the required focus. The *vocalizations* of the SB path ensure the focus won't slip away.

Hands-Separate Practice

For most people, the conscious mind can only concentrate on one thing at a time. But since the pianist plays with two hands doing similar activities simultaneously, in order to give the mind sufficient time with the muscles of each hand, he could begin the practice one hand at a time — hands-separately — which he begins to do when he writes his preferred fingerings above all the notes. After writing out the fingerings, he then continues to hold his focus by verbalizing the name of each note and the number of the finger playing that note. If it is a chord, he'll say the name and finger number of each note in the chord.

When he continues to practice hands-separately using the ST, he will begin to lock in perfect spatial patterns in each hand. When he puts the hands together, his muscles' memory of the spatial patterns may be established in both hands well enough to expedite the SB/ST practice.

Putting the Hands Together

Stop, place your fingers on the appropriate keys, then when you are sure you are feeling the correct key(s), and that they will be played perfectly including pitch, fingering, dynamics and touch, press them with the Singing Tone touch.

Play every note exactly like this from the beginning of the piece to the end, repeating nothing. When you have finished the piece once, put it away. It was perfect. No mistakes have to be corrected. The practice session is over for this piece of music today. Sleep on it. Tomorrow you will also do it once exactly the same way, and the same way the next day, the next day, and the next, until you reach a level of comfort that produces that magnetic pull to increase your speed. Do it, but remember *never faster than perfection will allow.*

If you have to observe these things for every note you play, it will be super slow, perfect, and anxiety-free.

In a few more days, you'll again feel comfortable increasing the speed without sacrificing perfection. Then a few days after that, you'll do it again. Keep up this pattern until your speed reaches performance level. Then begin the 15/15 sequence in preparation for performance (fifteen repetitions a day for fifteen days prior to the recital; (See Before the Performance, in Chapter One for the rundown).

Consistent Discipline

As mentioned previously, ST allows the piece to be learned without anxiety through slow, anxiety-free, focused practice sessions. There are consequences if you stray from this path. To illustrate this, I'll relate an experience that caused me to stop playing piano, almost for good.

At my college, instrumentalists were required to solo with the orchestra as part of the culmination requirement. I would be performing the first movement of Schumann's Piano Concerto in A minor. After that concert, I took an extended hiatus from the piano — that lasted twenty years. Here's why: somewhere during the preparation for that performance I did almost everything wrong. I had slipped into anxiety-driven, unfocused practices. I had lost the connection between my brain and my fingers, the connection Ethel had so carefully instilled in me. I had labored over passages I deemed difficult, and skimmed over the easy ones. And finally, I rushed to get the piece to performance level (no seasoning time).

I had taken a vacation from my studies with Ethel for the summer, but continued to practice the Schumann because I had the concert looming before me. My practice eventually evolved to a combination of Ethel's singing tone and entertaining myself. *When practice is entertainment, it erodes away focus.* When I returned after the summer, I played the Schumann for Ethel. She started to cry. Unfortunately, her tears weren't from emotion evoked by my passionate performance. They were from abject disappointment. By that time, *frantic* had returned to my performance. I had resurrected my old bad habit of *entertaining* myself when

I should have been starting each practice with Ethel's sharply focused Singing Tone. This meant that at anytime, I could lose control of the performance. This possibility was always looming in every practice session and I *knew* that it could happen during a performance as well.

Finally it *did* happen, and at the worst possible time. Concerto Night had arrived. It was the culmination of four years of music study. We had a famous conductor — the renowned violinist and conductor, Andor Toth. The orchestra was huge, my sister was the concertmaster and all these musicians would be there in support of me – the soloist. No pressure. We would be performing the Schumann. It was the last performance on the program. The last thing the audience would hear before going home. It had to be good. No pressure. So, there I was, armed with my iffy, unevenly practiced, frantic, passionate performance that I would be presenting to a packed house... no pressure!

Need I mention I was a wreck? I needed to hear from Ethel. So the last thing I did before the performance was to call her. Even though I hadn't seen her since I made her cry several months earlier, she was kind, and assured me I'd be fine. Then it was time.

I stood in the wings while the stage crew wheeled out the Baldwin Concert Grand piano. The lights came up and the conductor and I stepped out onto the stage. The piano seemed further away than it had seemed during rehearsals. The piano keys were brighter. There was a clarity about everything that I couldn't remember experiencing during rehearsals. When I sat down, I could have sworn the keys were swimming back and forth. I uttered a prayer, "God help me." The keys stopped swimming.

The audience waited. On the podium, the conductor paused, and then with one percussive move cued the crash of the orchestra's first chord and my frantic, passionate musical ranting began. Now, my heightened anxiety level was off the charts. The zone that I usually slipped into during my mindless practices had vanished. *I was totally awake now.* This state of alertness drove my tempos up. I felt as though I was dragging the orchestra behind me. It was like pulling a ship with my bare hands. My core was in chaos. A little smattering of confidence left over from the ST practice sessions floated by on that turbulent sea so I grabbed it like a drowning man at flotsam and rode it from one difficult passage to the next. On the more difficult passages, I was able to retain the focus of the ST because I'd maintained it throughout my practices. It was the easy passages that didn't get that benefit.

The movement is approximately fifteen minutes long; it was the longest fifteen minutes of my life. I would have nightmares about swimming piano keys for years.

Finally it was time for the cadenza – a portion of the movement where the piano is completely exposed because the orchestra stops playing – this is where the pianist is supposed to show off her technique for several pages. My fingers picked this moment to impersonate wood. But I charged through anyway, hoping my passion would win out over the wood. Finally came the trill which marked the end of the cadenza, the cue for the conductor to bring back the orchestra.

I was elated that I had survived the hard part. Now I could almost see the finish line. I could relax going into the final pages of the performance (I keep referring to "pages" but of course there were no pages – all the music is memorized) because that part of the music had never presented me with any problems. I was actually looking forward to it. Then suddenly it was ... *gone!* There I sat with my fingers poised *above* the keys, *not on them.* The orchestra kept playing. The conductor kept conducting. When he noticed I wasn't playing, he looked over at me as if to say, "Where are you?" I shrugged and once again looked to God. He came through again and allowed me to – in one last, desperate move – throw my fingers at the keys and finish the movement triumphantly with the orchestra. That day I "hung up the piano." In the aftermath, I learned that except for the conductor and me, nobody was aware of the debacle. We all finished the performance to thunderous applause. I wondered, however, if it was actually sympathetic applause. Then I bowed, shook the conductor's hand and my sister's hand, bowed again, and left the stage. The audience kept applauding, so I again stepped out from behind the curtain, bowed again, then tried to get the orchestra to stand and take a bow. They wouldn't so I just shrugged my shoulders, threw my hands at them in mocked disgust, then gave the audience a perplexed look. They laughed, I bowed again and left the stage — again. The applause finally died down.

Why?

In retrospect, if I examine my performance in light of Ethel's ST method, I surmise that my brain had disconnected from my fingers in the non-technical passages of the music. During my practice sessions, I had maintained the ST for the most difficult passage work because that was the only way to maintain evenness and perfection. I had spent hours on these parts of the piece, but for the easier parts, I simply played them through while my focus wandered. Consequently, these were the parts of the piece that caused Extreme High Anxiety (EHA) to rear its ugly head during the performance. (Note: I've coined the term EHA because I feel it is the only one that adequately describes what happens during these moments. Stage fright or the fight or flight response is insufficient, and mere high anxiety isn't strong enough.)

With the mode of practice I employed I had broken a cardinal rule of the SB method – *even practice* which had yet to be introduced to me. The fact that I was practicing eight hours a day didn't help when the practice didn't proceed with *all notes* given equal attention. The stark clarity of the concert stage caused me to focus on the less-practiced passages in a way I had neglected to do during my practice sessions. So my confidence, which had been so carefully nurtured by the ST practice sessions, wove in and out of my performance. In other words, I would own the stage for only brief passages of the music – the difficult ones — then it would own me for the rest. Fortunately the audience never knew the turmoil I was in because if nothing else my technique reflected my ST training so it was good, and my passion carried me through the rest of the way. But I shouldn't have had to suffer that much. Where was the confidence I thought I had during my practice sessions and during my rehearsals with the orchestra? Answer: it absconded during the attack of EHA because it was a false confidence. The true confidence was lost when I returned to my old bad habit of self-indulgent unfocused practice sessions.

Another Contributing Factor (Lack of Time)

Another factor that may have contributed to my confidence meltdown was learning the music too quickly. My first choice for my senior solo with the orchestra had been a Mozart concerto. It was performance-ready. But the conductor nixed it saying its transparency required a level of perfection that might challenge the orchestra. So I had to choose the Schumann which was not performance ready. There would be no time away from it. I would be hammering away at it daily, therefore — no seasoning time.

How did Ethel Know it Wasn't ST?

For years I mused about how Ethel could tell that I wasn't using her method of the Singing Tone on the day my performance made her cry. I finally decided it was my unfocused, labored, harried attack on the keys. It was a sign that I was using force to mask the anxiety that slips in when the ST is not adhered to. She could sense that I was only occasionally in control – that my confidence was sporadic, which meant I only intermittently owned the stage. With ST practice, the performer *always* owns the stage, it isn't sporadic. SB and ST practices and the confidence they inspire, more than anything, keep these unwanted anxious moments from occurring because once they do they weave themselves into the fabric of the music where they remain like a burr from a cactus – perhaps forever.

That forced, heavy-handed attack on the keys was, perhaps, Ethel's clue to my abandonment of the ST because ST doesn't require force. Since your core and fingers are producing the music, and since your fingers are already strong enough to accept any signal from your center, all the unforced power you need is already there. ST has made your hands and fingers strong. How? The musician plays millions of notes, each with an easy, comfortable touch radiating from his core. Trainers at the gym in my neighborhood concur that workouts for *building strength* rather than bulk, are generally characterized by a *lot of repetitions with light to medium weights.* So, unforced touch (light weights) millions of times (a lot of repetitions) builds the musician's strength. Now when the music calls for "loud" his touch is equipped to respond without artificial force because his hand and finger muscles are strong enough from all those reps to support the added power emanating from his core. All of this, of course, the controlled anxiety and the unforced power, come together when the key element in ST, *focus,* is maintained.

Ideas on Focus from Other Performers

During a recent interview on the Charlie Rose Show, the renowned actor Frank Langella said, *"Focus is everything!"*

He emphasized three major points: *Know the lines, know what they mean, and mean what they say.*

That was perfectly stated because these are the steps the practitioner of any discipline should adhere to. They immediately pull the focus to the point of the utterance of each word, the playing or singing of each note, the dancing of each step.

In his book, *On Piano Playing Motion, Sound and Expression,* famed concert pianist, Gyorgy Sandor wrote, "But the preparation – the innumerable hours spent practicing – must be purposeful, not automatic and mechanical, and it must be consciously controlled by the mind." He went on to clarify that we must know what we are doing while we are practicing because if we do not, we are wasting our time. Then he cautioned that this conscious focus can only last for approximately twenty minutes for most people, but that time can be increased with practice.

The SB path aids in extending this focus time by the student's stopping to vocalize — in the case of the piano student — the name and finger number of each note before it's played.

During a recent interview on the Tavis Smiley Show, Itzhak Perlman, the legendary violinist, said that *the music has to play in your head before you play it on your instrument.* He further clarified when he added that he has heard other performers relate instances where the *music (during their performance) occurred before they were ready.*

I took this to mean that the automatic music stored in their muscle memory took over and left the performer's focus behind. When you allow your fingers to play the passage without your focus, it becomes an *accident* that they are successful. If all of your practices were replete with *successful accidents* as well, imagine what will happen to your accidental successes when they are confronted with the stark clarity and muscle-freezing effect of EHA during a performance. Conversely, if the music occurs in your head before it is played, you were there first with your focus, on top of the performance, not behind it. You retained control. *You owned the stage.*

Revisiting the Piano

Did I go back to the piano? Yes, briefly, twenty years later when my eldest son, Robbie, and I played three performances of an arrangement written by my husband, Bob Smale, of excerpts from George Gershwin's *Rhapsody in Blue* at a college show. Robbie inherited his father's ability to play piano by ear. He played the second piano part, which he learned by just listening to his father play it. He would depend on his ear to get him through the performance. I, on the other hand, am totally dependent on the written notes. Of course, there were none. All of the music was memorized. Since I had learned the Gershwin piece *before* studying with Ethel, when I regurgitated it, it came complete with my old anxieties. I did, however, apply the ST to ensure perfection, but my anxieties remained. I had once again started to practice with my old bad habit of self-entertainment. Due to this, I fooled myself into thinking I had overridden the anxieties because I sounded fantastic during these self-aggrandizing practices. I hadn't. Once again, my performance was passionately frantic as I steamrolled my way through to quash the anxieties. The ST practices saved me by allowing perfection to dominate the performance, but I was in turmoil the whole time.

Note: I neglected to mention that it was for these reasons that I had given up all my pre-Ethel music. I felt that regurgitating old music would resurrect old bad habits.

The audience loved our performance of Rhapsody in Blue as well they should have, because my son did a masterful job, and I managed once again to fool everybody but myself. So remember, if anxiety was present in the initial learning of old music, it may return.

Practice Makes Perfect if the Practice Was Perfect

A fellow student knocked on the door of the practice room where I had been working out my issues with the piano. The college had installed a large number of these cubical-sized soundproof rooms, complete with upright pianos in the new music building, and I took advantage of one daily.

I answered the door. A nervous young man entered and began explaining his reason for the interruption. It seemed the college orchestra was going to perform *The Carnival* (popularly known as *The Carnival of the Animals*) by the French composer, Camille Saint-Saens, a humorous suite in fourteen movements for two pianos and orchestra.

He had been working on the second piano part and asked if I would consider playing the first piano. I jumped at the chance, because the music didn't have to be memorized.

Over the next few weeks I practiced the Saint-Saens alone. I didn't have any anxiety issues because, traditionally, dual piano music is performed with the sheet music in front of the performer so *that* immediately put me at ease. But apparently that concession wasn't enough to abate my counterpart's anxiety. He disclosed to me that his anxiety over performance manifested itself in a strange way. It seemed that he would have no memory of his performance after he left the stage. In fact, in an effort to minimize his anxiety, he had chosen not to play the first piano part hoping that decision would take the audience's focus off him and put it onto the pianist playing that part. In other words, he wanted to hide yet still be a participant in the concert. In retrospect I surmise that his performances may have been relegated exclusively to his muscle memory with little or no active focus.

We began our first rehearsal together on the big stage in the auditorium because that was the only place where there were two grand pianos. I found that in spite of his anxiety problems, he was an accomplished pianist, so everything went along smoothly until we got to the movement titled "Aquarium." About sixteen bars into the piece a debacle occurred — and by debacle, I mean a *train wreck*. Every measure was suddenly filled with dissonance. I had to shout at him to get him to stop playing. He didn't seem to realize anything was wrong. It was as though he wasn't listening to the music we were creating so he wasn't aware of the problem. He seemed to have zoned out. Now I understood what he had been trying to tell me about his mental state during a performance. But we weren't performing; we were just rehearsing. Apparently, in his mind, he was performing because he wasn't alone in the room. Maybe I was making him nervous, or perhaps he was imagining an audience filling those empty seats in the vacant auditorium.

We finally figured out that he had skipped a measure and *that* caused the problem. So, we went back and started him on the road to relearning that passage and putting back the missing bar. But try as he did, the culprit kept disappearing. Just when we thought the problem was resolved, it would pop out again. Why? Because he had practiced it that way. Old habits are hard to break.

Finally, the day arrived. It was showtime. The house was packed. I looked at my co-conspirator's anxiety-ridden face. Its green hue told me that my attempts at calming him hadn't worked. Then, the house lights went up and the performance was on. The orchestra was in rare form. Our concert grand pianos filled the auditorium with Saint-Saens' clever musical recreations of animal sounds. Everything was going great — until the "Aquarium." The culprit — that elusive measure — *took a vacation again*. Now the auditorium was suddenly filled with *cacophony*. The ethereal tones of the "Aquarium" movement had morphed into chaos. But true to the performer's creed – "The show must go on"— we all charged our way through the calamity as though it wasn't occurring. Of course the second piano part ended one bar ahead of the rest of the music, but I don't think my partner was aware of it because we didn't stop to correct the mistake as we always had when it occurred in rehearsals. I never mentioned it to him and he may not be aware of it to this day. The good news is that the rest of the performance was wonderful. It was as though we all rallied to make the music so amazing that the audience would forget the fiasco they'd just heard. It must have worked because we concluded to resounding applause. Or might it have been sympathetic applause?

This was an example of what happens when practice is not perfect and anxiety-free. His problems with anxiety could have been greatly ameliorated if not solved with ST/SB practice, and if he was calm throughout his practices, he surely would have caught the elusive measure.

The Recital's Job

It is almost impossible during a practice session to create extreme high anxiety (EHA) by simply envisioning an imaginary audience. Here the performer is only entertaining himself with visions of an audience completely enthralled with his performance. All he is doing in this scenario is wasting time because he is expecting this same sensation during the real performance when in fact the sensation will be far more intense than he expects. Better to have a series of recitals in front of actual audiences to be better prepared for the shock of the EHA. This is why many teachers hold multiple workshops and recitals. In either case, if the practices have been ST/SB, the student has a much better chance of weathering the performance storm.

This Approach

This approach to practice with its total focus solves several problems the performer has. The first being *mistakes*. They're gone. During the performance the student will find he literally can't make his fingers make a mistake. They just won't go there. The next thing that happens is that the EHA (stage fright) comes under control. The student will find his focus can keep him too busy to bother being frozen with fright. If the anxiety does anything, it will simply drive his tempos up but it won't interfere with his control of the performance. Then there is technique. ST/SB practice unleashes all the good technique that was always there hidden under layers of self-doubt. With this level of focus the muscles relax and absorb the music during practice sessions, and then release it during the performance.

Final Analysis

The sum of the parts makes up the whole. The parts of my musical training came from the myriad of teachers I studied with, some of whom taught using drills designed to strengthen fingers — gymnastics for the fingers. Then there was Ethel whose method minimized the effects of anxiety by forcing a focus that yielded perfection and connected the body, mind, and soul to the music.

So I've basically gone from *making* my fingers work to *allowing* them to play the music. Which approach is the most important? Can I say I could have done without either one? Probably not, because I didn't. But I know that Ethel was a renowned artist with her method, and her anxiety-free practice approach levels the playing field for all of us.

In the final analysis, I believe *it is easier to take less of too much than to contend with more of not enough.* So the power and strength is there if you need it, and from that position you can choose to back off and *feel* the note while you connect to the music.

I'm grateful for both approaches. Can I say that training the muscles gently will accomplish more and allow the student to go further than forcing the muscles to respond through vigorous exercise – when I did both? No. It wouldn't be fair for me to make that assumption when I've had the benefit of both. But I can say that without the intercession of Ethel's method, all my powerful training would have come to naught. I had hit a wall, reached a plateau and wasn't going any higher. The ST method opened the door to the real focal point: the music.

The name of the game is *faith.* Have faith in your ability, faith that your body is ready to produce the end product. The SB/ST practices establish that faith so *your brain knows your muscles are ready and your muscles know your brain is ready.*

Q. & A. (Answers to the most frequently asked questions)

Resurrecting Old Music

Q: I've been trying to relearn Claude Debussy's "Clair de Lune." Unfortunately the fingering I once used has been lost. Now relearning it is going extremely slowly because I've written in new fingering which has to be changed whenever my subconscious remembers the old fingering. This happens a lot. How can I speed up the relearning process?

A: Well, it looks like you have discovered that whatever way you originally learned the piece, that's the way your muscles will replicate it when you try to relearn it.

My suggestion is to treat this old piece as if it were a new piece. Put the music on the stand, check the key and time signatures, and everything else, and then verbalize as per the SB method in each practice session. It is so slow that you avoid creating those anxiety-filled moments that the anticipation of mistakes creates. If the piece was learned perfectly and without anxiety the first time, it should come back that way. Don't rush to relearn it. Students often experience that magnetic pull to go faster as soon as the music is only barely in their muscles. When they give in to this urge *to go faster than perfection will allow,* this gives rise to an anxiety that causes them to *expect* mistakes to occur – so they're constantly waiting for the other shoe to drop. And when it does, they can take solace only in knowing they weren't blindsided because they *knew* a mistake would occur. But *why* did it occur? Because they were *going faster than perfection would allow, and they knew it.*

After that, the musician starts the mistake-correction cycle. He first has to erase the mistake's sensation in his muscles and his memory, then he has to erase the anxiety the mistake caused. This is harder than it sounds because the mistake is like the *wound* and fixing it will leave a *scar* — the anxiety that went along with the mistake. Whether the mistake does or doesn't continue to pop up during subsequent practices and performances, the anxiety (scar) may remain. So, resist sliding into the beautiful ethereal tones of Claire de Lune. Be dogged if necessary. Vocalizing the information about the note should sharpen your focus. Do this for as many weeks as it takes to retrain the brain and those muscles to work together.

Again, since your muscles will eventually recall the sensation of the piece the way you learned it the first time, the old fingerings will continue to resurface. Unfortunately, that's not all that will resurface. If you learned the piece with mistakes and anxious moments the first time, those will resurface as well.

My suggestion: Why fight an old fight? If the music you are trying to relearn wasn't learned perfectly and without anxiety, forget it. Learn something new perfectly and without anxiety. There is so much beautiful music to choose from. If, however, you enjoy fighting old battles over and over, then by all means, go for it.

Childhood Ability

Q: I remember being able to perform music so much sooner when I was a child. But around the age of twelve, I started to lose that ability. After twelve, I started *thinking*. And that interfered with my ability to just allow my muscles to handle the performance.

I remember an episode in particular that let me know that ability was slipping away. I was twelve years old and I thought I was ready to perform Beethoven's *Minuet in G* in the next recital which was a week away. I had learned the piece in two weeks, which wasn't that unusual. I felt I *knew* it because I could *play* it. On the day of the recital, I very confidently sat down at the piano and promptly began playing the *Minuet in G — in the wrong key.* I don't remember what key I was playing it in, but I knew it wasn't in the key of G when my fingers were functioning in an unfamiliar pattern. (Not having perfect pitch, I wasn't able to *hear* the correct beginning notes in my head before I began to play them). After a few more unsuccessful tries, my teacher finally made his way up to the piano, and calmly placed my fingers on the correct keys. Then, even though feeling totally embarrassed, I was able to play the piece through to the end. Why did this happen?

A: Around the age of twelve, a child's brain starts crashing the party with heightened self-awareness. The ease with which he was former-ly able to learn the music is now being challenged. This heightened self-awareness also causes a heightened awareness of the things and circumstances around him, which, in performance, manifests as EHA.

In their book *To Learn With Love*, written as an aid for parents of Suzuki music students, Constance and William Starr relate their own experience with their son, who prior to the age of twelve had always approached his performances with confidence that bordered on noncha-lance. But at twelve his budding self-awareness awakened and threat-ened to derail his ability to perform. He came off the stage with tears in his eyes stating his disbelief at his never-before-experienced level of nervousness.

All teachers of adolescent students know of the turmoil that these stu-dents are experiencing. But during the performance the student himself suddenly is made aware of it in a most dramatic way. We teachers wrap it all up in a neat little package and we call it *nerves*. But we now see it may very well have biological origins and implications that begin at the onset of puberty and continue throughout life.

The "why" for the unsuccessful start would be that you were not aware of the new development in your maturation. You had abandoned the music to the muscles and the subconscious mind. You were expect-ing to perform the piece mindlessly after only two weeks of practice, just as you had been able to do in the past. But now, with this added brain interference, you would have to approach your practices differ-ently. The ST/SB practice sessions will, again, *level this playing field*.

The "why" for being able to complete the piece without further in-terruption from the brain was because you probably consciously dis-missed it and left the rest of the performance to your muscle memory.

If you haven't given your conscious mind enough time with the music during the practice sessions, *you'll surely hear from it during the per-formance*.

The Goal
Q: Should the musician's goal be perfection?

A: No. The goal should be creating beautiful music. Taking the ST/SB practice path will lead you to perfection with minimum anxiety.

Perfection is one of the gifts of the ST/SB.

ST/SB and the Artist
Q: Does the artist need to use the ST/SB method?
A: On some level the artist may already be using the essence of ST/SB. However, he has the ability to climb *his* ladder to perfection much faster than the student. Perhaps he is able to gain perfection the first time he plays a piece of music, using superior sight-reading skills, well-honed focus powers, and a well-developed ear. So the contemplation and preparation for each note is so much faster than that of the student that it isn't even discernable.

A case in point: Cinda Redman, a friend who is a concert pianist, is part of a dual piano team that performs all over the world. She can, metaphorically speaking, read *flyspecks*. Her superior sight-reading skill led her to her career as a concert pianist. Along with her unbelievable reading skill, came superior focusing skills, the key to ST's success. Improving reading skills is possible, perhaps through familiarizing oneself with musical styles and patterns in the music over the years, but at Cinda's level of expertise, this acquired ability has to have been coupled with an innate gift for sight-reading: People tend to pursue careers that center on their inborn talents.

Another case in point is that of my husband, Bob Smale. He was best known for being a member of the Lawrence Welk Orchestra of which he became a member in 1969 and remained until the show went into re-runs in the 1980's. (Note: The Lawrence Welk TV Show is one of the longest continuously-running TV shows on earth. It is now at sixty-one years and counting.) Bob was, to quote his peers, a "musician's musician." He graduated Phi Beta Kappa from the University of California, Berkley, with a major in music and a minor in English. He conducted, wrote, composed, or wrote arrangements of music for such notables as Donald O'Connor, Vic Damone, Kay Starr, The Mary Kaye Trio, Lawrence Welk, and Matt Monroe to name a few. He was a musical genius. But his genius lay in *creating* music. He didn't teach because – as he put it – he couldn't communicate what was happening in his head to another person. In his one-man shows, he would – while he was on stage and in front of the audience — instantly create and perform an entire piece of music out of three or four random notes offered up by members of the audience. He could look at an orchestral score and hear all the music on the page in his head. When he wrote, he did it in a room without a piano. He didn't need it because he could hear what he was writing in his head. He just *did* it, and he'd been doing it since the age of three. But he was predominantly a performer. And because his creative juices were always active, he was always thinking with his conscious mind. This active conscious mind caused his focus to be acute. This focus is the key to the success of ST/SB practice. So his performances manifested the perfection and anxiety-free essence of the ST/SB practice.

Cinda and Bob were both professional performers who reached great success from different directions – Cinda through her exceptional reading skills, and Bob through his creative skills – but both of them gave, and Cinda continues to give – total focus to every aspect of the music. In both cases, their special gifts served to *expedite* their performance-readiness. They could, at least theoretically, be ready to perform a work the same day they received it.

The average student may not have these or other innate abilities, but that shouldn't hold him back. Remember, the path that SB/ST provides will level the playing field and give him the tools he needs to reach levels that will astound him. It will take longer for him than for someone with such special abilities, but success is attainable if he stays on the path.

Scales and Arpeggios

Q: Are they necessary?

A: The piano student learns most of the patterns his fingers will eventually be required to play from the numerous pieces he plays. But the playing and eventual mastery of scales and arpeggios have a positive affect on his confidence. It makes him *know* he can perform anything the composer throws at him. If the student is plagued with uneven scales, he needs to stop and apply ST to every note. If he keeps it up, he starts to notice that an awareness of each key will remain no matter how fast he plays the scale. His focus has morphed into an awareness of the touch. Then he'll come to realize that he can't make a mistake with this level of awareness of each key. He will have uncovered the secret. This awareness and perfection push his confidence to higher and higher levels. He is in control. He'll feel like he has caught the brass ring of perfection.

Note: It makes a huge difference if you remember to *begin every practice session with SB/ST*. So if you begin each practice session with scales, then SB/ST the scales before playing them up to speed.

Patterns

Q: I know there are patterns of finger activity that all instrumentalists develop over the years. Since most of these patterns are already established in my muscles, why do I have to waste so much time with ST practice on those familiar passages?

A: Remember the piece of music is a unit. If your muscles are trained in the whole unit evenly, when EHA strikes, your brain won't panic; it will *know* your muscles can handle the storm, because they were SB/ST trained on the *whole unit — evenly*.

As you've pointed out, patterns develop in the muscle-memory of the music student, patterns that keep recurring in subsequent pieces and become comfortably familiar. Each new piece, however, will be made up of both familiar and unfamiliar passages. When the familiar passage occurs, the student may have a tendency to abandon the SB/ST. Now his focus lessens while his speed increases through the familiar passage. But then he comes to an unfamiliar passage and he stumbles. This stumble-point may weave itself into the fabric of the music. From this point, he either slows down drastically, or he stumbles through the unfamiliar passage at the too-fast speed leaving a myriad of mistakes and their respective corrections in his wake. Even though he may eventually succeed in correcting all the mistakes, that stumble-point may always arouse anxiety which could have been avoided if he'd stayed with SB/ST. That would have allowed him to painlessly segue from the familiar into the unfamiliar passages and maintain the continuity and unity of the piece.

Sight Reading and Performance Pieces

Q: Should I sight-read a new performance piece before I start practicing it with the ST/SB?

A: No. Since ST/SB is used when the student is striving for *perfection in a performance piece*, he should not sight-read his way through it even just once. The ST/SB starts on day one. Don't practice your sight-reading on your performance piece. If it isn't music you are familiar with, you will only look over the measure you are about to play to observe rhythms in your head, and then you'll ST/SB each note in that measure. Your reading at this point is only allowing you to observe the rhythm in your head, while you prepare your muscles and brain for the focused, anxiety-free perfection in the execution of the note or chord you are about to play.

Chapter Three – Martial Arts

A Focused Mind-Muscle Connection: Stop Bow for Martial Arts

Our family's introduction to martial arts came early and out of necessity. Back when our son, Robbie, was five years old in the first grade and younger than the other children, we discovered he was being bullied. Imagine that — six-year-old bullies. When my husband found out about it, he rushed out of the house, grabbed the culprits and marched them back down to the school and into the principal's office. In those days, school administrators weren't taking that proactive position against bullying that some are today. This principal mirrored the times and did nothing. In retrospect, the principal's failure to get involved was probably the right approach, because after my husband's interference, the bullying got worse. Our next move was to attempt to arm our children with the necessary skills to stop the bullying themselves — by enrolling them in a martial arts class. We chose a Korean style, *tang soo do,* taught at the Tarzana Karate Studio under the direction of Master Dennis Ichikawa because we were very impressed with the high-energy classes we visited. It was evident that strength, confidence, and discipline were being instilled in the students and it was all being done in an atmosphere that combined fun with success.

Eventually it worked. The bullying stopped. The years passed, and one day my daughter, Margaret, was unable to continue with her already prepaid classes, due to an unrelated injury. Master Ichikawa suggested *I* take Margaret's remaining classes. I looked at my body and decided it did need some work, since I had recently given birth to my third child. Perhaps I also thought of it as a legitimate way to escape all those diapers for an hour or so, three times a week. So, I agreed to finish out the year with my daughter's classes – with no intention of making a thirty-five-year career of it. I just wanted a few moves that would serve me well in case I was ever attacked. Instead, I became addicted!

I'd never had so much fun, or worked so hard. The experience was not only life-changing, it was mind altering. Two years and nine months later I was testing for black belt. Receiving it marked another defining moment in my life.

Tae Kwan Do

It was later, when a friend opened a *tae kwon do* studio (The American White Tiger with the famous Grand Master Park on staff) that the owners offered me a teaching position. I was tempted, but knew that I'd have to earn a black belt in the new style, and among the requirements was learning ten new *katas*. I needed some way to learn those *katas* perfectly. That was when desperation gave me the nudge to employ Charl Ann's SB practice method. This would be my first attempt at knowingly using her SB practice path. Her method would ensure anxiety-free perfection in my practice sessions. And since I couldn't afford to unlearn mistakes — invariably those mistakes crop up under the stress of the test — I tailored Charl Ann's Stop Bow Method to fit my *kata* practice. That meant that instead of stopping a bow to focus, analyze, and contemplate, I'd be stopping my whole body before every move. Then I'd have to make my focus dictate every microsecond of every move in the *kata*.

A *kata,* sometimes called a *form*, is a solo, choreographed fight with an imaginary opponent. It looks like a dance with attitude. It is to a martial artist as a piece of music is to a musician. It's made up of powerful moves, both offensive and defensive, using feet, hands, arms, knees, elbows, head, etc. The moves collectively resemble a fight against an invisible opponent. Since I already had a black belt in *tae kwon do's* mother style, *tang soo do,* I only had to complete the learning of the *katas* along with some other requirements to be ready for black belt testing. Daily I followed Charl Ann's dictates of stopping to analyze each move –its motivation, its power source, its position on the mat, its stance, etc. – before ever moving to execute the move. Then, the actual move would be so slow that it looked as though I was standing still doing nothing. That was the pattern of my practice daily. Initially it took a great deal of time, but not nearly as much time as it would have if I had to correct mistakes. My ultimate success made me a believer in the method. I now believe it could be extended to include almost any physical activity where the practitioner seeks anxiety-controlled perfection in performance. This opens the field dramatically to include sports and dance.

Why does this method of practice work so well in the martial arts? The short answer is that there is no wasted time in your practice because every move is totally focused and perfect. We see this focused practice in the popular martial arts style *tai chi*. It is perhaps the most recognizable of the martial arts if for no other reason than it is practiced so slowly. Because of its slow practice, this style has world-wide appeal, because almost everyone can participate. No move is more difficult than any other when they are all delivered in slow motion. This *forced focus* approach applied to every move ensures success at whatever stage the practitioner is in. I've come to view the *tai chi* method of practice as the martial arts equivalent of Stop Bow. Before using the Stop Bow Method for my martial arts practice, I had to learn by stumbling around in the mistake-correction no-win cycle.

Do We Learn From Our Mistakes?

Before being promoted to the next level, *tang soo do* students are tested in front of a black belt panel. The first half of the test consists of a series of *katas* (forms)

The *katas* are cumulative, so by the time you are a black belt candidate, you are required to perform all ten forms from the first basic form to the black belt form. The white belt student only knows one form – basic form number one (spelled phonetically, *giecho hyung il bu)* — so that's what he or she does. It goes without saying that most students are nervous in this situation, with all those accomplished black belts there to evaluate them.

But nerves alone couldn't have accounted for all the breaches in technique I committed on the *kata* the day I took my first test as a white belt testing for my first colored belt. Some of the judges' comments on my performance were:

a) Back leg failed to lock out in your front stances;

b) Folds (position of the hand or foot just before it strikes) weren't deep enough;

c) Punches spun too much or not enough;

d) Elbow was over-extended on punches;

e) Yells were too weak; etc.

It was both mind-boggling and disappointing.

Over the years I attempted to correct these breaches in technique. But try as I did, they continued to creep back into my form. Why? My answer is simple: I had actually *practiced* those mistakes, over and over again. Every time I practiced the form mindlessly, I was solidifying those mistakes in my muscles' memory. All the passion in the world can't fix bad technique. I passed the test and received my next belt, but only because as a white belt I was only *required* to get all the steps right in the form. In other words, my feet and hands were where they were supposed to be when they were supposed to be there. But the fact that the judges mentioned these mistakes meant that even as a white belt there were some attributes in the basic techniques that should have been a part of my focus. Even during my black belt test almost three years later, there were still elements in that *kata* that I wasn't happy with. So, what have I learned from my mistakes? I've learned *not to make them.*

It wasn't until fifteen years later, after I had moved on to other styles of martial arts and after I had quite literally forgotten that first form — which is essential if you are going to relearn the form from scratch — that I finally applied my sister's method and relearned that first basic form. Of course by then I would be approaching the form from the perspective of a black belt. That meant I would be seeking perfection at a different level. But then the Stop Bow practice means perfect, focused practice at whatever stage of development you have attained.

Using the Stop Bow Path
Since this initial practice is from a black belt's perspective of a white belt level *kata*, the SB examination of the situation will be done a great deal more scrupulously. While the white belt only has to be concerned with the steps in the *kata* and focusing in on the moves at a rudimentary level, the black belt, on the other hand, should be concerned with every aspect of every move he makes – what motivates the move, what will create the power he'll need for the move, what will give him the speed he'll require for the move, what will put him where he needs to be to perform the move, etc.

A Black Belt's Perspective on a White Belt *Kata*
Katas have a special purpose. They are designed to teach the body to move intelligently in a confrontation. It takes several of the techniques that the student has learned independently, and puts them together in context. In it the student now performs his blocks, strikes, or kicks in different directions while his body moves across the floor in pursuit of the perceived attacker. The black belt must keep that first *kata* in his repertoire of performance *katas* because tests are cumulative. The black belt candidate must perform all ten of them, and his performance of all the beginning and intermediate *katas* is expected to have dramatically improved. So here is the black belt's approach up to and including his first strike against the attacker.

The Look
From his attention stance in which he connects to his core, the black belt senses his attacker's approach on his left. So the first move is *the*

look. It can be either ostentatious or surreptitious. For the sake of show-biz, he may pick *ostentatious* so when he *sees* the attacker, the audience believes him. Some martial artists may disagree with the reference to show-biz, but over the years I've found that just skillfully performing the *kata* by itself will not result in winning the division at a tournament. There is another ingredient necessary to boost the performance over the top, and that ingredient, a high-energy focus, first manifests itself in — *the Look!*

For this look, your connected body and mind turn to focus on the opponent. Every split second of this move is driven by that high-energy focus. Here is your first opportunity to *take the stage*. Every eye in the house should be riveted on you because of the smoldering power of your focused *look.* In other words, don't throw away this first move. It is much more than simply turning your head to see your opponent. It must come from your core, so your entire body is alert during the course of that *look.* The move into that first look should be exaggerated with show-biz flair. In order to accomplish this, the practitioner should study every nuance of the initial look made by competing champions at tournaments. See what's happening with their shoulders and hips before their head, with hair flying, comes to rest with their eyes piercing the eyes of the opponent. That eye-piercing, high-energy focus never abandons the performance — it's maintained throughout every move.

Note: *Performance* implies *show biz.* In a real situation, however, the look will occur surreptitiously. For a woman, she must maintain her element of surprise because unless she is a body builder, she doesn't have the muscle-strength of a man. Therefore, if her initial response fails to render the assailant helpless, she doesn't have the option of duking it out with him. So, in a real situation, her response has to be completely covert. She must both sense his approach, and see him with her peripheral vision. If she makes a big show of seeing him, she's lost her element of surprise.

The Low Block

Now the attacker's powerful front kick is approaching. The black belt's first move — after the *look* — is a powerful low block to divert the attacker's kick. It is delivered at the end of a quarter turn to the left and completed in a left front stance (left leg is forward, knee bent with 60 percent of the body weight on it. The right leg is in back and straight bearing 40 percent of the weight.)

The black belt should ask during his SB practice, *"Where will that power come from?"* Answer: from six sources: the pull of the pulling-hand, the centrifugal/centripetal force of the blocking hand, the pivot of the hips in the quarter turn, the lock out of the back leg in the left front stance, the tightening of the stomach muscles, and the expelling of the breath, and all of these movements are *core generated*.

Here is the description of that move. Initially, your weight is evenly distributed on both feet. At this point your *look* has let you know your opponent is about to deliver a powerful front kick, so your block needs to be low which means your fold is high. But your feet need to maneuver your body out of the line of the opponent's kick while positioning yourself to deliver the maximum power in your block. At the moment of impact, you will be in a left front stance.

Now for the details on how you are going to make your feet and hands deliver you to the target on time with power. Again, read through the next few paragraphs even if martial arts doesn't apply to you — to get a sense of the focus, preparation, and attention given to each nanosecond of the move.

After the *look,* you'll find that in order to get off your opponent's line of attack, you'll have to address a weight shift. First, shift your weight to the right foot to free up the left for the left front stance. At this point you've already folded with your upper body because now speed is of the essence. The fold is the coiling of the body in preparation for the strike. Another word for the fold is *chamber* or *cocking* which comes from gun vernacular. In this case, the strike is a block. It has to be delivered with enough power to deflect the opponent's powerful kick.

"If the opponent's kick is powerful, you have to redirect it powerfully," said Grandmaster Dennis Ichikawa.

In order to get that maximum power in your block, you'll be delivering the block with the following moves being performed almost simultaneously: a pull of the pulling-hand, a pivot of the hips, the swing of the blocking hand aided by centripetal force, an expelling of the breath, a tightening of the stomach muscles, and the lock-out of the back leg — all core generated.

When the block is completed, 60 percent of your weight is on your forward leg.

All this description is to explain the mental and physical processes that the black belt should be addressing for just this one move. All this analyzing before the move pulls the focus into every split second of the move. So the slow performance of each of those actions ensures the perfection of the move, generates energy, produces power, and locks the move into the muscles and the brain.

Then you stop before going on to the next move, doing the same thing again: analyzing the move before slowly and perfectly executing it. Then you stop again and repeat the same process for the next move, and the next and the next until you finish the form. Don't repeat anything. Every move was perfect. Stop the practice. Sleep on it (seasoning time). Tomorrow repeat the practice — again only once — exactly the way you did it today; stopping before each move to ensure every nanosecond of it will be perfect by the time you complete its execution. Sleep on it again. The next day, repeat it again exactly the same way - only once. Sleep. Keep up this pattern of practice for a week or two before you do any increase in speed. But with that increase, you will *only go at a speed that will ensure perfection and maintain your focus.*

When the form is finally up to speed, the moves will be crisp, independent, and on purpose.

In an effort to keep from boring readers unconcerned with the martial arts, I'll stop here and simply reiterate that if the activity you are performing is ever to reach perfection, your practice has to be perfect from the very first time. Remember, there are no mistakes. None. There are no *repeats* to correct mistakes because there *are no mistakes.* Don't even entertain the thought of a mistake. Think before you act. If you know that you *only have now* to do it right, you'll focus in on it and *do it right the first time,* no matter how long it takes. If you were observing this extremely slow practice, it would look like the practitioner was simply standing there doing nothing. Don't worry about how slowly it goes at first, because if it's right the first time and every time after that, you will eventually attain speeds that will astound you. All the preparations for the move, the weight shifts, the fold, and any other aspects of the move will seem to disappear. To the casual observer, it will appear that the strike was just suddenly there, that nobody saw it coming.

Making the Connections

After the tae kwon do studio closed, I moved on to another style of martial arts — *hapkido.* This style borrowed the best techniques from multiple martial arts – kicks from tae kwon do, hand techniques and holds from aikido, and various weapon practices from other martial arts styles – all of which appealed to me. I chose this style and most particularly, this studio, because Master Fariborz Azhakh is one of the best martial artists in the world. Just *watching* him perform is an education in itself. He owns whatever stage he is on. And, as all great artists do, he continues to train with his own masters. Under his tutelage, the students become excellent competitors. He is a champion and he passes his amazing technique on to his students.

One day Fariborz asked if I would give him some piano lessons. I had stopped teaching piano years earlier because it was fatiguing listening to excuses about why students hadn't practiced. But here I agreed to do it because he is a disciplined person and I knew he would practice diligently, making it worth my effort. After a few weeks of lessons, I told him about my sister's Stop Bow Method, and how I'd used this method in the past to perfect performances in other disciplines. He listened politely.

In *hapkido* class a few days later, he instructed the students to line up along the walls. Then he proceeded to have us do one of our most basic moves, the back kick. After he concluded that some aspects of the students' kick needed improvement, he set about correcting it in the most precise way. He went down the line dissecting everyone's kick, having the students hold their positions while listening to a description of the next infinitesimal portion of the kick. We all then moved very slowly, with very tiny moves into the next part of the kick. The entire kick should take less than a second, but here it was going on for ten minutes and the kick hadn't as yet been completed. He was correcting even the tiniest imperfection of the kick *before* it was executed. He wasn't going to allow them to practice it less than perfectly, even once more. He was putting better technique into the kicks in the *slowest and most precise way possible*.

Now I cannot say for sure that my comments about the Stop Bow Method resulted in this approach, but I know he was listening and *that* is the mark of a true master teacher: Listening 360 degrees, learning from everyone, and applying everything he learns.

Pointers from the Dancer

A friend, Marian S. Weiser, was — for forty years — the head of the dance department at Pierce College in Woodland Hills, California. She gave some insightful pointers from the point of view of a dancer. Her key point was *energy*. She never allowed it to fall. And her *energy* manifested itself as *passion*.

She maintained that dancers are among the greatest athletes in the world. The dancer's body is the instrument through which he sings. A *good* dancer has a well-honed body, trained in the dance genre in which he performs. A *great* dancer adds that last element – passion-led energy. He or she is a master of maintaining this potent energy level throughout the performance. This energy emanates from a core that includes the entire torso – the abdominal muscles, the ribcage, the solar plexus, etc. — and feeds this energy to every extremity of the body.

The technical aspects of the moves in the dance are paramount, but *passion-charged energy* drives each one. This energy is electric — it reaches out from the stage to impact everyone in the house. This energy is so potent that it is felt even when the performer is standing still. Marian said that "the audience will – if that energy is maintained – become one with the dancer." They'll feel the emotion, the focus, the drive, the power, and the energy. She also said that *the look* of the martial artist becomes *the feel* or the *passion-driven energy* of the dancer.

Some critics may call this dancer's display – charisma. The author of *The Charisma Myth*, Olivia Fox Cabane, says this charisma is attainable. In other words, the performer does not have to be born with it. The martial artist performs his *kata* – a dance with attitude — with this same potent energy. To it, he has added the *unseen opponent*. Now he becomes not only a dancer, but an actor as well. When he "sees" his imaginary opponent, he has to be so focused, so convincing, that his audience "sees" him as well. This energy drives both the dancer and the actor. Now his SB practice has to include, not only every micro-second of the move, but the focused, motivated energy of the move as well. The good news here is that one of the by-products of SB practice is the *creation of energy*.

Think *Camera*

Another dancer and friend, Ernie McDaniel, added that the dancer has to have every nanosecond of his dance perfect in form, focus, and energy. It has to be so perfect that it stands up to the scrutiny of the film of a 16 mm movie camera. The old 16 mm movie camera's film actually has tiny frames each of which is a picture visible to the naked eye. If you film the *kata,* each tiny portion of every move will appear on the film strip. Imagine taking each of those frames and making an eight-by-ten glossy print of it. Would the dancer or martial artist be comfortable showing *all* of those glossies to anyone? That is the essence of stop bow practice. Is every tiny bit of the move perfect in its focus, form, and energy?

In order for each part of each move to be perfect – with all of these elements in place – the practitioner must be aware of them during all of his practice sessions. Imagine just how slow that practice has to be to incorporate all of these elements into each fraction of a second of the move.

More Good News

The good news is that this super slow practice only has to occur once today, once tomorrow, once the next day, etc. for however many days it takes for you to reach the level of comfort that lets you know you can handle a slight increase in speed without creating anxiety-producing mistakes. I was always amazed at how much my muscles retained with that super-slow, focused practice, even after so few focused repetitions. Even though the moves are in extreme slow motion in the initial *kata* practices, they will be — when ultimately performed up to speed — crisp, independent, on purpose and so fast that to the spectator they will look as if they materialized out of nowhere.

Aikido

Eventually, Aikido beckoned. I had already been introduced to Aikido from Master Fariborz, so I assumed it would be an easy segue toward the black belt in this soft style. It wasn't. Every teacher has his own path to perfection in his style of martial arts, and Sensei Jun Mateo was no exception. It was here, in these practices, that I saw what can only be described as the true essence of SB. Every move was analyzed. The footwork was scrupulously drilled into us until we *felt* the laws of motion at work. Every move was meticulously choreographed to ensure perfection in every nanosecond of the move. And the moves were always in context. That meant every time the move was performed it was with both an attacker and a defender so the student never lost sight of why he was performing the move. It was a long and often painful road. With all the interruptions in my studies of the method, it took seven years to earn the black belt.

Aikido allows conservation of movement and energy. Its timing requires precision because it allows the opponent to get close enough for the defender to direct the opponent's momentum. It makes use of the part of Newton's first law of motion that states *things in motion tend to stay in motion at the same speed and direction.* So Aikidoists don't impede their opponent's momentum, they simply aid him in defeating himself by allowing him to continue on in the direction he was already headed but faster than he was expecting to go. This conservation of movement and energy allows the practitioner to store the energy so he can use it in the *hold* that will render the opponent helpless. There are no punches or kicks in traditional Aikido. Thus meticulous attention to every detail of every move is monumental. This is the SB path.

In Summary

The key to a perfect, energy-driven and confident performance remains the perfect practice of the SB path. It will keep the performer focused and present for every move. The TV and film actor Wilford Brimley once gave some words of advice to my husband that apply perfectly here. He said, "You don't have to ski down the whole mountain; you only have to ski on the snow that's *under your skis.*"

Q & A
Depletion of Energy

Q: If so much energy is being expended during the performance, what keeps it from running out before the performance is complete?

A: *The Stop Bow Does.* Keep in mind that every practice session should begin with SB. This practice is extremely slow because you are required to stop before each new motion is made or before each note is played or sung. The stop itself creates energy because, while stopped, you are holding your position and contemplating the next move. This generates heat, acting somewhat like a slow warm-up before a hard workout. *This stop and subsequent holding of your position is the energy creator.* Each time you stop throughout the piece, more heat is produced, and that accumulation of heat preserves the user's energy throughout the entire practice session. If your last practice just prior to a performance is a SB practice, you will have enough energy to sustain the performance as well.

15/15 Countdown to Performance Rule

Q: The 15/15 practice rule: How stringent is this rule?

A: This 15/15 regimen may be too strenuous for some more active art forms like some forms of dance or for more lengthy pieces of music like a concerto. In these cases, the 15/15 regimen can be amended to include fewer reps per day, but for more days prior to the performance.

Imaginary Audience

Q: What is so bad about imagining you are performing in front of an audience when you are practicing?

A: Even if you are only imagining an audience, you are hampering your focus. You may simply be drumming up a false anxiety situation that you believe mirrors the anxiety of the actual performance. It doesn't. When you are actually confronted with the real performance situation, you'll be shocked to find the anxiety you were drumming up doesn't come close. So all you were doing was wasting valuable time. Time that could better have been spent in focused brain-muscle connected practice. Avoid the urge to *entertain* when you are practicing. Your practice should be a private thing between you and the work you are doing, not between you, an audience (real or imaginary), and the work.

We were all watching Sayed practicing his form. He was one of the black belts in the *hapkido* studio. Whenever he practiced, every eye within viewing distance would be riveted on him. There was something about Sayed's practice that captured the attention of the onlookers: it was an acute muscle-connected focused power emanating from his inner core. He was totally absorbed in becoming one with his form. He wasn't performing. Instead he was privately (in his own mind) creating a work of art. His form displayed the essence of SB practice in its focus and definition. Even when he practiced slowly, every nanosecond of his moves showed a deep energy driven focus. He never lost sight of the fact that he was there to practice, not entertain.

SB and Hard Style vs. Soft Style

Q: What martial art category is best – soft or hard style?

A: Both are extremely effective against an attacker, especially if the practitioner has adhered to the SB path. The hard styles stress aggressive kicks and punches, while the soft styles use the opponent's own momentum coupled with disarming holds to defeat him. After studying three hard styles, I went to a soft style. For me the hard styles built strength, flexibility, speed, confidence, and a competitive spirit. The soft style drew it all into perspective because it taught the student to work close to the opponent using precisely choreographed moves, balance, momentum, and timing.

But Which Style Will Preclude the Need for the Other

Q: Is a hard style all-encompassing enough to preclude the need for a soft style?

A: A man always has his muscles to fall back on, but a woman has to get it right the first time. She has to depend first on her intuition to help her avoid confrontations, then on the element of surprise to allow her to render the assailant helpless immediately, and lastly, on her training. If any of these three are compromised, she doesn't have the muscle mass (unless she's a body builder) to fall back on. I am a woman. So I found I needed both of these categories of martial arts to be well-rounded.

If, however, I were to dissect the two and analyze what I gleaned from each, I'd have to say that I found the anxiety flare-ups that occur when pitting force against force (hard style) may defeat the victim before the assailant even gets to her. The style that will calm the extreme anxiety this situation causes would be the soft style. But then I would have to ask: what follow-up will allow the intended victim to be the last woman standing? To that question I would have to answer: a hard style.

Whichever style you choose, the SB is the practice method that will zero in on the details, create perfection and confidence, control anxiety, and allow the style to do what it was designed to do: protect the practitioner.

Regarding Bullies

Q: Should a school administration be proactive or not? The proactive approach sometimes appears to makes the situation worse.

A: These days the administration has to take a proactive approach or risk being accused of negligence, but today's proactive approach can take many different forms. It doesn't only have to be punitive because when it is, the bully tends to subsequently *make his victim pay.*

What causes a person to become a bully? Evidence is substantial that bullies are people whose self-esteem has been damaged. They appear to need to transfer their own hurt and humiliation to others by bullying them. They may be constantly on the prowl for potential victims to boost their own self-image, so vast numbers of people experience being bullied every day. But the young child is the most vulnerable. He may feel that there is no help coming to his aid. I experienced this as a child.

It was during the summer school session while I was standing in line waiting to go to class that it happened. A large girl approached me. She started loudly threatening me. I was perplexed wondering what she was talking about. Even at my tender age, I recognized that she had no provocation for her assault. She was simply showing off for her friends by threatening someone younger and weaker than she was. She ended her verbal assault by loudly informing me and everyone else that she was going to beat me up after school. I was terrified. I went to every adult I could find throughout the day seeking help. No one would take me seriously. It was as though the adults felt that a child's problems were small because the child was small. When the bell rang at the close of school, I dreaded the walk home. I knew the bully would find me. I also knew that the only help I would be getting would have to come from *me*. I dejectedly walked down the steps of the school praying as I went. I then spotted a tree with a low hanging branch. I reached up and tore it off. The branch in my hand was almost like a little bit of company: with it in hand I didn't feel so alone. Now when the girl approached me I was standing there armed with my pathetic branch. She looked over me and my branch. Then she yelled out, "Hey girl, did you say…?"

"No," I said with as much confidence as I could muster. Then she looked again at the branch, mumbled something, and walked away. She never bothered me again.

From that experience I've come to surmise that a bully's potential victims are those he or she presumes to be weak. Then why did she pick me? Probably because my general demeanor smacked of victim.

If, however, that victim suddenly appears capable the bully may back off. I had armed myself with that flimsy branch which must have given me at least a modicum of confidence, because she never approached me again.

How much better it would be if the potential victim never assumed that victim persona in the first place. Decades later in my self defense classes, I taught that the first line of defense for a potential victim is to *not look like one*. Stand up straight with shoulders back, stay alert (*focused*), exude an attitude of confidence, and use good judgment because a pity-party attitude is an open invitation to the bully.

Chapter Four – Teaching: Mathematics and Drawing

Evolution of the Stop Bow Path for Math

Unlike the performing arts which require the muscles in our bodies to be trained in tandem with our brains, math only requires the training of our brain. However, like the performing arts, we will need to build confidence. We do that by building on solid and strong — not tenuous — former knowledge. If all the former knowledge has been gained honestly — built on what we've taught ourselves — we will have a solid foundation on which to build higher mathematical knowledge. Then we'll be confident with the new knowledge. We will have taken the *math stage.*

The beginning math student is typically in preschool. His curriculum is very simple. He uses small numbers and if he uses them enough, he starts to memorize addition facts, and multiplication tables. If they were simply memorized, however, with no understanding of what these facts *really* meant, the knowledge built on them would be tenuous. Is it a good idea to memorize the facts and tables? Of course it is. But when will the student be able to build successfully on this memorized knowledge as he would have to do in higher mathematics? The answer is — when he begins to focus on its true meaning. When will he do this? When he *needs* that knowledge. It may take years, or it may never occur at all. Officials who dictate curriculum are finally beginning to realize that pontificating teachers only allow learning at a very superficial level. True learning only takes place when the student grinds it out for himself. For me, it took going back to the most rudimentary levels of math.

I was a college graduate with a minor in math but I felt my math knowledge was as tenuous as my early piano knowledge. I wasn't happy with it, so I started *teaching myself math.* Teaching yourself is the quintessential way to learn. You are introduced to the knowledge by your teachers, but the actual learning takes place outside the classroom when you are alone. There you have no one to depend on but yourself. That is where you dissect what you "learned" that day. Then you analyze it, internalize it, synthesize it, and draw it on paper until it makes concrete sense. Only then will you gain the confidence that allows you to own the knowledge and be able to build on it.

It was the 1970s. By then, I was a mother with two small children.

Perhaps I felt that my brain needed more challenge than child-rearing was providing me. So while I was fixing meals and changing diapers, I was asking myself the most basic math questions possible, questions like, "What does the number three *really* mean? Is it a noun, or some other part of speech? Doesn't it depend on where it's used in the sentence? Should we be talking about sentences in mathematics? What does multiplication mean? Does three times four mean the same thing as four times three?" It took forcing my brain "muscles" to reexamine each operation (addition, subtraction, multiplication, and division) and view it in a deeper way. In other words, I was getting rid of tenuous knowledge built on shaky basics, and replacing it with concrete, provable knowledge, built on solid basics. My number one question was becoming — and remains — W*hat does this <u>really</u> mean?*

Here is an example. To find the area of a circle, we use this formula: the area of a circle equals pi times the radius squared, which tells us the area of a circle *is the same as* the area of pi (A number that is slightly more than 3) times the radius of that circle squared (which means actual squares whose dimensions are a radius long and a radius wide). This formula tells us how many of these squares we can fit inside that circle — 3.14 of them. What does this really mean? First you have to realize that it's hard to measure the inside of a circle — to find the number of square units that will fit inside it because we measure things with rulers that have straight edges. These rulers are only adept at measuring things that also have straight edges, things like walls and floors and squares. But circles have round edges, so the inventor of this formula said to himself, "Okay, let's find something else whose area is easy to measure. But it has to be related to our circle." He chose squares. But these particular squares are going to tie into our circle because they will have sides the same length as the radius of our circle. Since he chose to take the radius of our circle and build the squares on that radius, they would be a radius long and a radius wide. He then proceeded to see how many of them it would take to fill up the circle. He managed to cram 3.14 of them into the circle. So, he found that the area of a little more than 3 squares, each measuring a radius wide and a radius long, added up to the same area as our circle. (That number: 3.14, is probably the most recognizable number in mathematics. It is such a special number that it was given a name, pi, and a symbol, π. And for the purist, we must mention that this number goes on forever to the right of the decimal point. But it is still just a *little more than 3*). Another interesting aside: 3.14 is also the number of diameters that fit into the circumference of a circle.

A good project would be to take two different colored pieces of paper and cut one into a circle and the other into squares that measure a radius by a radius. That means you'll have to measure the radius of the circle and cut the squares to measure that radius long and that radius wide. Then glue the squares into the circle adjacent to each other and each with one corner at the center of the circle. Then cut off the remainder of each square that falls outside the circle. Take those pieces and cut and paste until all the pieces fit into the nearly empty quadrant on the circle. When the project is finished, you'll again see the same circle, but its color will have changed to the color of the squares.

So, you take each word in the formula, dissect it, draw a picture, and internalize it. If you do this, you'll come to realize that the formula is actually a sentence packed with important information. Now that you know what it is actually telling you, you won't just be taking someone else's word for it, you'll know it works because you've proven it for yourself. And you'll never forget the formula and what it means because you have this vivid picture in your head of those 3.14 squares being crammed into the circle. Now you'll feel confident with the knowledge. You own it, and now you can build on it. In retrospect, I realize that this was my Stop Bow Method for math — focusing on the most basic element, the *word*, then analyzing and picturing that word in order to fully understand what is being conveyed.

Taking a Lesson from Video Game Creators

In 1996 I began working as a math teacher in the Los Angeles Unified School District. My school was a middle school in the San Fernando Valley. Most teachers know that the majority of students don't automatically share their enthusiasm for the courses they teach, and that keeping students interested means making them successful. But how do you do that? It was a daily struggle for me. In an effort to zero in on what sparks their enthusiasm, I began concentrating lessons on *concepts* that could be drawn out in picture form, rather than just *processes:* lessons like the *area of a circle*.

But times had changed so much that simply adding a little touch of concept to the lesson didn't help keep the majority of students focused enough to be successful. Our students are being sucked into the entertainment vortex provided by the tablets and omnipresent smartphones. The teacher can only compete if he, too, jumps on the bandwagon. How? Perhaps he could begin by examining what the creators of video games, the kings of entertainment, are doing.

I posed the question to my brilliant seventeen-year-old grandson, David. After giving the question some thought, he enumerated several magnets that attract players: fun, cumulative achievements, rewards, global competition, camaraderie, 24/7 availability, and fame.

So to compete with these games, the teacher would have to build into the curriculum many little opportunities for incremental achievements. Then we'd have to design rewards that would accumulate, and add an element of competition; we'd have to make it available 24/7; it would have to have opportunities for camaraderie and teamwork; it would have to be fun; and it would afford the student the opportunity to become famous among his peers. To incorporate *all* of these attributes into our curriculums would be a daunting task.

Like the video game creator, Dr. Suzuki has created fun opportunities for the music student to succeed, which causes the student to *want* to focus so he can experience more success. The camaraderie comes about during the orchestra rehearsals and performances, and if the student excels at the highest level, he may become famous.

Charl Ann's method likewise creates fun opportunities with a combination of the Suzuki program and her fiddling program, so the students *want* to focus so they can achieve ongoing success. And to these fun opportunities, Charl Ann has added the time saver — Stop Bow, so perfect for today's fast-paced world where every activity has to be completed in record time. So, we have the fun; the cumulative smaller successes that lead to larger ones; the camaraderie; the expanded acclaim; rewards (accolades for winning competitions); and around-the-clock availability (the instrument is always available). So music teachers pretty much have it covered. But now we come to mathematics. How are we going to market math to our students?

Marketing the Mathematics to Students through Drawing

We could, perhaps, create math games. But they tend to morph into gambling. What else?

One day, out of complete desperation, an idea surfaced: What about drawing just for the sake of drawing? Drawing was something that the majority of students liked to do. Drawing was something that could be done within the confines of the classroom. And drawing was something that could incorporate mathematics. Why not? After all, the famous artist, Leonardo da Vinci, was also a mathematician. If *he* found the connection between math and art, one truly must exist.

I had been drawing *for* the students to illustrate concepts, but now I would teach *them* to draw using concepts. So, out of our marketing list, *success* and *fun* were chosen to spur the students on.

To do this, the students were armed with pertinent information about each line they would draw which included its size, shape, and location, and employed words from the student's math vocabulary, words like *diameter, horizontal, vertical, quadrant, line, parallel,* and *ellipse* – to name a few. If the line couldn't be explained in math-based words, it didn't appear in the picture. When we finished the first drawing, we had a picture of two tin cans.

What had prompted this act of desperation was seeing students with limited math ability entering my classroom at the beginning of each school year, sadly confident that nothing would change, that this year would hold yet another opportunity for them to be forced to demonstrate their ineptitude – another year of failure. It was obvious that they were intelligent because most of them were bilingual. What they needed was one tangible academic success. If they could gain success at even one thing, it would give them a foothold to build on. I knew most students enjoyed drawing because I had been confiscating their surreptitious artwork for years. In retrospect I realize that they *wanted* me to catch them drawing – they would *forget* to cover it up when I walked by — because it was the only success they could truly take ownership of — even at the risk of chastisement. Now, instead of all this drama, the drawings would be out in the open because they would serve a purpose — connecting something they enjoyed to something they needed.

So began Math Drawing sessions – one focused line at a time, slowly building the complete drawing. The meanings of the math terms were firmly locked into the students' brains because they had to use them to draw the picture. At the end of the session, each student had a product he or she could be proud of.

Even students for whom drawing was a challenge were successful, because the drawings were accomplished one focused line at a time – call it *Stop Bow for Math and Drawing.* For some of these students the sessions ushered in a new success mode that made a positive difference in their lives.

Stop Bow for TV Math Show Performances

One day, perhaps on the strength of these math drawing sessions, vice-principal, Brenda Winter gave me a flier announcing a call for teachers to participate in a local TV show called *Homework Hotline*. It took me three months to respond to the call. I finally got up enough nerve to phone the station and talk to the producer who subsequently asked me to come in for an interview. I did, and was hired.

My job was to teach math to seventh grade-level students on TV. Every other week I'd prepare a lesson that was in keeping with the standard we were teaching that week in our classrooms, and I'd present it live for the TV audience. I had been doing this for about a year when one day, right in the middle of my presentation I heard one of the cameramen yawn. It suddenly struck me. *I was boring.*

It is amazing how things happen in concert. The great yawn and Halloween occurred in the very same month, and all the teachers on the show had decided to do their next show in costume. How fortuitous this should happen right when I was feeling a burning need to spice up my act.

For years I had watched Homework Hotline. It was an award-winning show that did exactly what it was designed to do, help students with their homework. And it did it well. It was video taped live at a TV station in downtown Los Angeles. At one time the show employed a large number of teachers to take calls from students. The cameras would pan across the panel of teachers intermittently so the TV audience could see the teachers taking their calls live. The combination of live performances by the presenting teachers and the enthusiasm of the teachers on the panel taking calls, created an electricity that helped drive learning. We were doing the show live, but it was taped so it could be played in other time slots. I know this because one day I was walking past the waiting room in the Kaiser Medical Center and I just happened to peek in at the TV in the waiting room, and there I was teaching something I'd taught live three days earlier.

Eventually, however, budget cuts drove the show to limit the number of teachers on the panel to a fraction of what it had been. But the show was still cutting-edge. Teachers were still watching the show to see what the TV teachers were doing to motivate students in their subject. (On each show there were three presenting teachers; a math teacher, an English teacher, and a science teacher. This lineup changed from time to time to include other subjects, but for the most part it remained the same.) Students were watching to get help from the panel of teachers – or perhaps they were hoping to get mentioned on television. It was in the midst of all this positive learning that the cameraman let me know with his yawn that my part of the show was sadly in need of a makeover.

So now I would have the opportunity to spice things up, perhaps long enough to pique the TV audience's interest in the math lesson of the day. I was excited. I took the teachers at their word and wore my silly court jester costume for the Halloween show.

I drove to the studio in full costume – makeup and all. When I walked into the studio, however, and saw the other teachers, a wave of humiliation swept over me because none of them dressed in what I considered *a costume*. Their idea of a costume was a funny necktie or a colorful vest... and there I stood in my funny-looking monstrosity. *I was devastated.* I had to either do the show in my costume or my underwear. I had nothing else.

Luckily I had been practicing a little skit to go along with my jester character, and the host was a quick study and fell right in with the mood of the skit. My mood, however, was charged with humiliation and now with a bit of anger as well. When my part of the show was over, I simply left the studio. I didn't want to risk being berated by the producer in front of the other teachers. That night I played the tape of the show – my husband taped all the shows for me – and steeled myself for the debacle.

It never came. In fact, it was the *best* show I'd ever done. I learned a very valuable lesson that day. I learned that *the camera picks up the electricity in your mood*. I was angry and apparently that anger created the electricity that charged my performance and that made it come alive. So, for the remainder of the three seasons, I tried to re-capture that electricity by teaching every math lesson *in character* and *in costume* and did my best to charge my mood with fun, excitement, and enthusiasm, all of which I hoped would keep the students from switching the channel. Most of the time it worked.

But this new approach to the TV math lesson came with a whole host of problems. Instead of just thinking like a teacher, I had to think like a performer as well. At first, I ignored that aspect of the show. I simply entered the studio on show day, put on my costume and make-up, and proceeded to wing my way through the lesson. Well, something happens when the red light on the TV camera comes on, and it's just you and thousands of viewers. Extreme high anxiety (EHA) sets in if you're not as well-prepared as perhaps you should be. I found a byproduct of this state of mind to be *extreme clarity*. Suddenly concepts become crystal clear and you realize which part of the concept has been confusing students all these years. This revelation would be wonderful at some other time, but now, with the cameras rolling, it's too late to incorporate it. If you try to weave the information gleaned from this new-found realization into your ill-prepared presentation, you run the risk of going off on a tangent and your presentation can spiral out of control.

The upside of these terrifying moments of clarity was that those insights could be used in subsequent shows and it made me realize I'd have to make some changes. It was simply too hard to allow EHA to continue to drive each show.

So, I started writing out each show, complete with situations, costumes, and characters to go along with the concepts in the math lesson. Now I'd have to actually rehearse the character part while I wove it into the development of the current math concept. Now *time* became an issue because by the time I'd completed the writing and mailed the copy to the producer so he could alert the sound man, I was down to four or five days to learn my lines, and my character, and the props and processes for the lesson. My only choice now was to use my sister's Stop Bow Method to get me through each show. When I rehearsed, it was one focused word at a time. Preparation for that word included mental questions. What is my focus? Where are my feet, hands, gaze, props, etc.? I knew that only correct practice would bring about a perfect performance. I could only work at a speed that would ensure perfection: SB for TV Math Performances. What drove the need to employ this innovative process was a powerful fear of losing concepts or character on live television.

That's Fine for My Performance, But Was I Forgetting the Students?

There was one thing missing with this TV education, however. It is generally passive, a one-way conversation. Even if I was conversing with a live student on line, as I generally was, I was asking leading questions that led him or her to the correct answer. In other words, no real learning was taking place. My focus here was on *my* performance and what Stop Bow was doing for me. I needed to get back to the at-home student.

One day the producer asked me to fill in for another math teacher the *next day*. I didn't have time to prepare a character-driven skit to go along with the lesson, so I asked if I could teach one of my math drawings, instead. He looked reticent at first, but finally agreed. The next day I taught the very first *Math Drawing* lesson on *Homework Hotline*.

It was so well received that over the next two years I taught other Math Drawing lessons. When I did, the viewers learned to draw perfect pictures with slow, focused, math-based instructions. There were no mistakes because the pace was slow and deliberate. No line in the drawing was more difficult than any other line, and each word in the instructions was designed to evoke *focus* from the viewer. Each Math Drawing session began with a skit to draw the students into the mood of the lesson. For instance, to draw the picture titled Roman Arches, I portrayed Julius Caesar's mother-in-law who, because her chariot kept getting stuck in the big wash in front of her house when it rained, wanted the Senate to grant her permission to build a bridge over it. Of course she had to present them with a drawing of the bridge she intended to build which she proceeded to draw for them with her quill on parchment, using her yak-hair string compass to create the semicircular arches. Each line of the drawing was explained using math terms before the line was drawn. Then she'd wait for the senators (student in the studio who was demonstrating for the overhead camera, and the viewers at home) to complete the line. So the drawing progressed slowly and with focus, and developed perfectly, line after line, until the drawing was complete. We were using the Stop Bow approach for the Math Drawings – on TV.

The feedback I received from other teachers was that their favorite shows were the Math Drawing shows. They began urging me to include the math drawing lessons in a book, which I did. We are now in the fifth edition of the book. It is titled *Math Drawings: Good Stuff for Teachers, Parents, and Students* and is available at **www.mathdraw ings.com**. So once again, the Stop Bow path pushed the envelope to bring about perfect performances from the students.

In her book *The Charisma Myth,* author Olivia Fox Cabane – a must-read – points out that the main language of the brain is imagery. She says, "When you speak words, the brain has to relate the words to concepts, and then translate the concepts into images, which is what actually gets understood." Then she suggests that we speak directly in the brain's own language — pictures.

Of course she was referring to visual metaphors for impact, as she pointed out that Steve Jobs illustrated when he introduced the iPod Nano by pulling it out of the smallest pocket in his jeans, visually driving home its tiny size. But, this imagery serves us here in the math drawing context as well because instead of *conjuring* up pictures to understand the words as we do with metaphors, we are going one step further and creating *actual* pictures to understand the words.

In Summary

Just as the SB path for the music student directs him to maintain his focus through *verbalization* of the name and direction of the most basic element (the note), the math student's SB path likewise directs him to maintain his focus through *drawing* as per the dictates of his most basic element (the word).

The SB-like path to focus is the key to complete understanding for both the teacher and the student because the method forces the practitioner to seek out the core — the most basic element of a subject. In mathematics, the method manifests itself in the *search* for the meaning behind its most basic element: the *word* that accompanies the number. He finds it by questioning everything in solitude and worrying the subject until it issues its answers. Then, after all the *why* questions have been answered by the practitioner himself, and all the information has been analyzed, synthesized, and internalized, he will be able to communicate his newly-acquired knowledge in the language of the brain – pictures. It is because the language of the brain is *pictures* that metaphors are such a powerful tool. If you can draw it, you own it.

Chapter Five – Science Opinions

Why Does the SB/ST Practice Work?

Is there scientific evidence that explains this phenomenon? I went online and Googled this question: "Why is it that we benefit cognitively by our mistakes, but the cycle of mistakes and corrections hinders our physical performances?" The response was something on the order of, "That's a good question. Give us a few days to come up with an answer." A few days later, I nixed the question because when I reexamined it I realized it was a loaded question. I was *assuming* we benefit cognitively from our mistakes and that we don't benefit from the cycle of mistakes and corrections in our physical performances.

My assumptions were based on experience and observation. But sometimes they can paint a faulty picture. I observed that whenever I made a mistake on a test (cognitive) that I didn't make that same mistake again. From this experience, one might assume that I learned from my mistake. But did I? This experience didn't teach me how to fix the mistake, it only taught me not to make the mistake. Fixing the mistake would only come through true learning of the material: slowly and with focus, building on solid, previously-acquired knowledge (SB for mathematics).

Teaching your muscles to perform, however, is another matter. Now it's not just cognitive. Through the experience of countless performers and teachers, we know that in the case of performance only perfect practices can result in a perfect performance. When practicing performance pieces, we don't have the luxury of making mistakes and then going back to correct them because this pattern of mistake/correction can too easily morph into a cycle that is very likely to surface during the performance. What has science found that might back up this assumption?

It is common knowledge that when we do something physical – walk, type, play the piano, sing – our muscles retain a memory of that activity and the more you do it, the better the muscles remember the activity. Of course this muscle memory could be a combination of muscle and brain, working together. But I digress. The amazing thing is that the muscle or muscle-brain connection remembers the activity *for life*. That is why one can still ride a bicycle after not having ridden one for generations, or likewise, play the piano, after not having done so for decades. Why is this true? What does the scientific community say is happening during these muscle-building processes?

An article from *Science News* points to recent studies of this phenomenon done by researchers led by Kristian Gundersen, a physiologist at the University of Oslo in Norway. They also point to an article reported online August 16, 2013 in the *Proceedings of the National Academy of Sciences,* which explains what is happening when a muscle is being trained. It seems that memory in the muscle is being stored as DNA-containing nuclei. These nuclei proliferate when the muscle is exercised. But when the muscle falls into a state of atrophy, these nuclei don't die off as was previously thought. Because of this, these muscles retain a *memory* of their former fitness, even if the muscles wither from lack of use. Gundersen went on to explain why the nuclei proliferate during the muscle-building process. He points out that, "muscle cells are huge, and because they are so big, they need more than one nucleus to supply the DNA templates for making the large amounts of the proteins that give muscle tissue its strength."

The study also said that this is the reason a bodybuilder who allows his body to sink into a state of disrepair is able to rebuild muscle and bring his body up to its former level very quickly, much faster than any fledgling bodybuilder can build *his* body to the same level.

Good News Bad News

That was the good news. The bad news is that this muscle memory can work *against* a performer as well. The muscles may remember a mistake even if it is corrected. If they do, when the performer repeats the piece, the mistake is very likely to crop up again. After that, the mistake-correction cycle may weave itself into the muscles. Even if the mistake is eradicated, it may leave the performer with a residual anxiety that will be hard to erase.

Also, it may prompt the performer to try to leave his performance exclusively up to his muscles, leaving his brain behind. He may surmise that if the muscle has a memory of the move, one could simply store the appropriate moves there and zone out during subsequent practices. Of course that means his performance will be unfocused and perhaps dull. Remember that with SB, even though the muscles will eventually produce the music automatically, *focus must drive those muscles.* Dr. Suzuki said to train the muscles until they automatically produce the music, even when the musician is otherwise involved. He felt that the musician should be able to carry on a conversation while playing the music. This will ensure the muscles are ready. If, however, the music was focused when it went into the muscles then, on some level, it will still be focused when it comes out in performance.

The Stop Bow Method of practice ensures the muscles are ready and that your mind is *confident* that they are ready. This confidence puts you in complete control even when extreme high anxiety (EHA) rears its ugly head.

The Brain's Role in Performance

Glen Doman, the developer of the *Better Baby Course* says "Every baby is born with more potential than Leonardo da Vinci ever used."

In her book, *Drawing on the Right Side of the Brain*, Betty Edwards writes about scientific findings concerning the brain. She writes that scientists have known for more than a hundred and fifty years that the left hemisphere of the brain controls the language capabilities of most people. She notes that more recently scientists have discovered the function of the right side of the brain. For years it was thought that it had no particular function. Now, however, they've concluded that the right side is the subjective side. The left side is verbal while the right is nonverbal. In addition, they've found that there is a thick nerve cable called the corpus callosum composed of millions of fibers that cross-connect the two cerebral hemispheres. It allows the left hemisphere to take the verbal information and pass it through the corpus callosum to the right hemisphere where it is translated into pictures or music or something of a higher, artistic, or non-literal form. However, the left side is dominant between the two sides, and may interfere with the work of the subdominant, more subjective right hemisphere. For most *artists* of any discipline, the shift from the left to the right side is something they can do easily. It may even be second nature for them. For the rest of us, we have to figure a way to *make* that shift occur.

Among musicians in the 80's, a story was going around about a famous jazz musician. When he was asked if he could read music (left brain) he answered "not enough to hurt me none." An analysis of that statement might be that his left brain doesn't interfere with the right brain too much because he limits the situations that would call forth the left brain – situations like reading. No shift is required if he simply stays in the right brain mode, which he can afford to do because of who he is – famous and successful. Most of us, however, can't afford the luxury of staying in right brain mode. We're busy with work and family and can only enter into our passion now and then. And when we do, it has to be entered through the back door (left brain) with reading or analysis and such. So we need to know how artists get to the point where they can easily make the shift to the right brain.

Sometimes it's easier to picture a concept in the negative to bring it into perspective. So, again, I have to call on my own experience to draw the picture. I harken back to the time when I experienced what I believe to be this shift — albeit a negative shift. It was just before my performance of the Schumann on that concerto night. I've already described in detail the circumstances surrounding the performance: Swimming keys, extreme clarity, etc. But now in the light of these scientific findings I've concluded that just prior to my performance in which I ostensibly would be using my right brain, I suddenly made the inappropriate switch to my left brain — my dominant hemisphere — which immediately began trying to interfere with my performance. Why did that switch occur? Answer: I was experiencing EHA and my left brain did what it is designed to do — come to my rescue. The left brain came to my so-called "rescue" with misplaced thinking that surfaced as I took my seat at the piano. This *thinking* only served to interfere with the job the right brain was best equipped to handle. This *thinking* should have taken place during the initial stages of the Singing Tone (Stop Bow) practices, not during my performance. During the performance, the only brain activity should be coming from the right brain. I recall making a conscious effort to slide into the right-brained *zone* I was usually in during my practices. That zone should be where everything comes together: the focus, the confidence, the energy, the passion, the perfection. (Unfortunately my zone tended to be mindless.) But the EHA was trying to keep that from happening. I was finally able to do it, but, unfortunately I experienced multiple shifts throughout the performance — into the zone, out of the zone. Thankfully almost nobody noticed. As far as the audience was concerned, everything was fine. But it was harrowing enough to cause me to quit piano for the next twenty years.

Extreme High Anxiety (EHA)

Earlier I wrote about extreme high anxiety (EHA). I experienced it during that Schumann performance, and in front of *Homework Hotline* television cameras. In the next chapter more episodes will be revealed.

First of all, what are these moments of EHA? Movie makers have now begun depicting the pivotal action scenes by slowing down the action (slow motion), and turning off the sound. Now, every second of that action is crystal clear.

Where did the moviemakers get this idea? Perhaps from the baseball player who, after hitting the winning home run, says, "The baseball was as big as a basket ball and it was moving so slowly I couldn't miss it." Or from the story of the father who watched helplessly as his toddler ran happily toward the end of the unfenced pier and there wasn't enough time to reach and save the child — but he did. Or from the onlooker who watched, powerlessly, as time slowed and sound abated during a potential drowning scenario. Or the soloist who, when stepping onto the stage, experiences a shockingly clear awareness that comes when time slows. So these EHA moments run the gamut. They can occur in all walks of life. I felt that the phrase *fight or flight* was too limiting, and just *high anxiety* wasn't strong enough.

In all these situations, *time* seems to be the common factor. Has time slowed, or has your acute awareness of the situation speeded up to unparalleled proportions so it just seems that everything around you is moving too slowly? In either case, the *focus* the SB path produces can be the calming factor. But, in every case, what drove that need for the calming factor was EHA.

Chapter Six – Extreme High Anxiety (EHA)

From the Victim's Point of View

EHA can be triggered by a myriad of causes. Some can be resolved through prior training and unassailable preparedness and some cannot. But the overarching thing that connects the EHA experiences, regardless of the source, is the perception of time slowing down.

Whenever I've spoken to people who have been the victim of a crime, they have invariably disclosed that they'd been somehow forewarned. They say things like "Something told me to lock that door," or "Something told me not to turn that corner." These were warning voices, that sixth sense we all experience at times. They are warning us of an impending hazardous situation. In all these victim-scenarios, the warnings were ignored. One of the byproducts of those focused martial arts practices (SB path) is *recognizing* that these feelings you are having are indeed warnings. If you believe that, then you can act to avoid the impending perilous situation. Note: avoidance is the key; it is the highest form of self-defense.

A pertinent aside: in the 1980's an amusing avoidance story was going around in martial arts studios. Whether it's true or not is debatable, but it should be. As the story goes, a late night talk show host posed this question to his guest, a martial arts grand master. "What would you do if you were walking down a dark alley at three o'clock in the morning and six thugs jumped out to attack you?" Without hesitation, the grandmaster calmly answered, "Grandmaster wouldn't be walking down dark alley at three o'clock in the morning."

In the '80s I was embroiled in the preparations for *tang soo do's* black belt test. But as invincible as I felt, reality was always looming nearby. That reality was the fact that no matter how strong and fast I became, I was still female. And most assailants are male. (Note: I didn't say they were men. A real man isn't a bully; he doesn't attack smaller, weaker people.) This reality forced me to supplement my martial arts training with a class in the use of Mace – a brand of tear gas, used before the introduction of pepper spray. In those days, you had to have a license to carry Mace, and you had to take a class in its use to be able to get that license. So, I had my license to carry the little canister of Mace that hung on my key chain.

It was about noon on this particular day. I had gone to the bank to withdraw two thousand dollars because my husband and I were going on a cruise. My husband was the pianist for the Freddy Martin Band during the Lawrence Welk Show's summer hiatus, and the band was the headliner on the cruise. The upside to being the headliner was that the band members were invited to bring along their significant others — free of charge.

Since my black belt test was imminent, I couldn't take time off for a cruise unless I continued to practice on the ship. It was no mean feat finding a solitary space on that ship for that to happen, but I did. I would be practicing alone every night on the upper deck in semi-darkness when the deck was vacant and the ship seemed to pick this time every night to roll over the ocean swells most vigorously.

Even though the cruise was free, there would be incidental expenses like tips and gifts. So, I withdrew the money and asked that it be converted to American Express Traveler's Cheques. But this bank – which was really a savings and loan — had only its own generic traveler's checks. I didn't want those, so I took the cash, stashed it in my purse and planned to go to another bank later for the preferred checks. I decided, in the mean time, to stop by the market. So, I climbed into my car and drove less than a hundred yards to the market, diagonally across from the bank.

In the market, I picked out the few things I needed and stood in line behind a gentleman who kept turning around and staring at me. I started to become uncomfortable thinking something was amiss with my appearance. Then he began making idle conversation. I soon noticed that each time he turned around to address me, he would turn back around and make eye contact with a large, bald, forty-something man through the store's large plate glass front windows.

The hairs on the back of my neck stood up. I was getting a warning. But I did what most people do at a time like that — tried to ignore it. But something made me still worry over the strangeness of the man's attentions. I had forgotten about the money in the bottom of my purse. But that same something caused me to remember it…and then it all began to make sense. But still I found myself doubting those warning hairs still standing up on the back of my neck. I was saying to myself, that there was no way they could know about the money in my purse, that it was just my imagination. After all, it had been in my purse less than fifteen minutes. How could they know? *But just in case it wasn't my imagination,* I decided to take the situation seriously.

After the man paid for his groceries, instead of leaving, he went to the window and just stood there again alternating glances from me to the man on the outside. It was becoming blatant. I'd have to be a fool to ignore these signs.

I had to do some thinking, and soon. By this time I was in full blown EHA — the *extreme high anxiety* that comes upon a person when she realizes *she is the target*. Time slows down, sound abates, and she is completely alone. It doesn't matter how many people are around you, you are still alone. First I thought about having the bag-boy walk me out to my car. I dismissed that immediately because he was about the same age as my eldest son, and I wouldn't want a hysterical woman putting my son's life in danger. Then I remembered the Mace on my keys. But that was risky if the wind was blowing, and I would have to get closer to the assailant than I wanted to. I finally composed a viable scenario in my mind.

I had paid for my groceries after making a comment – loud enough to be heard by the man at the window — to the cashier that I only had eight dollars to pay for the groceries so she should stop ringing up purchases when she reached my eight dollar limit. I was sure he heard my comment but he still didn't move.

So, I took a deep slow calming breath, put the key for the car *trunk* in my right hand — everything else —purse and groceries — in my left, and flipped the cover off the Mace.

When the market doors sprang open I breathed again, said a prayer, then quickly walked to my car, opened the trunk, threw *everything* inside, slammed the trunk, and stepped between the cars – but still within clear view of the market. I knew I didn't have time to open the car door and get in because I could see the big man who had been outside the windows barreling down on me so I simply turned to face him with my finger on the trigger of the Mace — trying to look as confident as I could by plastering a little wry smile on my face.

The man stopped abruptly right in front of me within six feet, and stared at me. I could tell he noticed the absence of my purse. Then his eyes traveled down to my finger on the trigger of the Mace. Shock suddenly registered on his face but I realized that it clearly wasn't a fear of me or my Mace when his eyes widened with terror and he began frantically twisting his head back and forth scanning the vast expanse of the parking lot. He seemed to be searching, searching back and forth across the lot for … what? I guessed the police; he must have suspected a sting operation because a split second later, he whirled around and charged back across the parking lot – nearly colliding with his accomplice who then removed all doubt that he was indeed the accomplice when he — after his brain registered what he was viewing — spun around and raced off, in the opposite direction. I got into my car — still shaking — and drove home. The avoidance scenario had worked thanks to the prayers and warnings. I never figured out how they knew about the money though. I did notice, however, an abrupt turnover of that bank branch's personnel shortly thereafter.

Does EHA Drive Time?

When I later examined the event, I surmised that I was in a state of EHA from the time the hairs first stood up on the back of my neck, to my leaving the parking lot, because the whole episode couldn't have taken more than five minutes. Either time had slowed to allow all the fear, resolutions, planning, prayers, and actions to fit within those five minutes, or the EHA had sent me into a state that sped up my thought processes and actions, so that it just seemed as though the time had slowed to allow it all to happen within that time frame.

Frozen With Fear (EHA)

One Sunday morning, while on our way to church, we spied a baby boy – a toddler — carrying a big purse standing alone on the corner of a busy boulevard, looking like he was about to launch into the street. I immediately pulled over and stopped. But we were on the wrong side of the street. I started praying that he wouldn't jump off that curb. As we were praying, we noticed another motorist — on the correct side — pull over. We continued to watch nervously as she got out of her car and proceeded to coax the child to come to her. She scooped him up and carried him to her car. And then they just sat together in her car – waiting for someone to come along looking for him. With the situation under control, we continued on our way. We only had two blocks to go to our church.

When we turned the corner, however, we noticed a sizeable group of people *running around aimlessly* in front of the church there. I had a feeling that this scene was somehow connected to that child whose life had just been saved by the Good Samaritan. So I called to them and asked if they were looking for a child. They shouted back, "Yes… yes!" So I pointed to the Good Samaritan's car. They all raced toward the car.

This was an example of what happens when people are crippled by EHA. Brains shut down and muscles react without purpose. The minds of these people were *frozen with fear*. They were running around in circles. This clearly wasn't accomplishing anything. But, who is ever trained for this scenario? Nobody. When it's *your* child this kind of news hits you differently than it does onlookers. But if the participants in this episode were interviewed, they'd probably say that from the moment they realized the child was missing, time slowed, and everything moved in slow motion.

About two years later, I had a similar situation. But this time I wasn't an onlooker I *was the mother* with a missing seven-year-old child. After that experience I would know the depth of the emotions of a parent of a missing child firsthand.

I was in class at our local college when I noticed my husband standing in the hall beckoning for me to come out. He looked worried. "David's missing" he said. "I think he's been kidnapped."

The full impact of what he was saying didn't faze me right away because I knew my husband tended to be an alarmist so I generally took his dire conjectures with a grain of salt. We went over his movements for the past few minutes.

He said, "I went to the karate studio to pick up David, but he wasn't there. I was a little late, but David knew to wait for me. I asked the owners about it but they didn't know anything."

We drove back to the studio and I rushed in and reiterated Bob's earlier question to the owners. Again they looked perplexed and shrugged. I was suddenly struck by the uncaring attitude they and the other adults in the studio seemed to display. Time was beginning to slow. I found myself making my way to the phone to call the police. Then the full impact of the situation hit me: my child is actually missing. Time slowed in earnest now. Nobody was doing anything to help. Everybody was going about their business — moving in slow motion. The class I interrupted resumed. I was completely alone with my worst fear. Images of terrible abusers began racing through my mind. I started pacing through the strip mall where the studio was. It seemed like an eternity since I had called the police. They still hadn't arrived. A feeling of abject helplessness permeated my soul. I called 911 again but this time I was screaming at the dispatcher. The police finally arrived. I was beside myself with fear. I yelled at the police officers for taking so long to respond. One of the policemen was belligerent, but the other seemed to understand my overwrought state. We told him what had happened. The policeman kept telling me that David was probably walking home. I kept telling him that couldn't be true because David was only seven, we lived more than two miles away and he would have to cross many streets, some of them multi-lane boulevards. When the policeman said the helicopter was scanning the streets and they hadn't spotted him, my whole body turned to ice.

Where was he? If the helicopter had scanned the area, surely they would have spotted a little boy in a white karate uniform walking alone on a dark street. The policeman told us to go home and wait. I couldn't go, but he told us that we needed to be at home in case David came home. Otherwise, he might wander around the neighborhood if nobody was home. It was dark and cold and I knew David didn't like his karate uniform and he always took off the top when he was outside the studio. That meant he was in a wet-from-sweat tee shirt on this cold November night.

My husband put me in the car and we drove home. When I tried to get out of the car my legs wouldn't hold me up. And when they finally did, I couldn't get my feet to move. I don't remember how I got into the house, but when I finally did, I dropped to my knees and began praying — pleading and making deals with God.

I had been crying out to God for what seemed an eternity, when the doorbell rang. My then nineteen-year-old son, Robbie, flew to the door and threw it open. He yelled, "Where have you been?" Then he vented by slamming his fist into the wall.

I thanked God, smeared away the tears that were streaming down my face, and stood up. By then David was stumbling through the doorway. I grabbed him and just held on tightly until he finally wiggled out of my grasp. We phoned the police and thanked them for their trouble.

A lot of conversation followed, in which David disclosed that he had indeed, walked home. After some prodding, we figured out why. He was in love with an older woman – she was ten — and she always rode the bus home from the karate studio. David wanted to impress her by leaving the studio when she did and perhaps walking her to her bus stop. This way he appeared more grown up. Then, to further impress her, in case she was looking out of the window of the bus, he proceeded to walk the rest of the way home. He didn't want to slink back to the studio in ignominious defeat to wait for mommy and daddy, so he just kept walking. Whenever he got to a big boulevard, he'd asked someone to help him cross it. He even asked a homeless man to help him.

That was my worst EHA moment. All my martial arts training

hadn't prepared me for that, because it wasn't a martial arts moment. It was a mother-and-child moment. So my body functioned the same way the bodies of those people in front of the church had — muscles responding ineffectually or not at all, brains not functioning, while everything around recedes into a lonely, soundless, slow-motion state.

Dr. Caroline Leaf, in her book, *Who Switched Off My Brain?* (another must read) writes, "...research shows that fear triggers more than fourteen hundred known physical and chemical responses." She then points out that when these responses happen, they throw the body into a frantic state because they activate a combination of more than thirty different hormones and neurotransmitters.

With all this going on in the body, it's no wonder time seems to slow down; it has to in order for all this to happen.

This whole scenario played out in less than one hour from the time Bob picked me up from the college to the ringing of the door bell. Did time slow down to allow all the anxiety to occur, or did my mind speed up and move so fast that it only seemed that all the things that were happening around me were moving in slow motion?

Can a Performer Use the Time-Slowed Element his EHA Produces to His Advantage?

We've all experienced these EHA moments, so we know how they affect the mind and body. Most performers, however, know that during a performance they want to either avoid these moments entirely, or use them to enhance their performance. How is it possible to do the latter in the middle of a performance? Perhaps by using the extended time that EHA evokes. Time appears to have slowed because the EHA is driving the mind to warped speed and this makes everything in the surroundings appear to be moving in slow motion. The mind perceives this as time slowing down. When it does, time is no longer an issue. It seems to be present in abundance. In fact, the performer may feel he has all the time in the world. He may even view time as being on his side. It's a trick but it can free up his focus to do what his SB practice has trained him to do. Now he can shift his mind's focus to his core that will signal the appropriate memory in his muscles that will produce the performance. His perception is that since the mind is connected to the muscles, and the mind is moving at hyper-speed, so are the muscles. The slowed time tells him that he doesn't have to push because he has plenty of time for his focused well-honed muscles to complete his performance.

How Healthy is EHA?

But is it healthy to allow the EHA to linger throughout the performance? According to Dr. Lissa Rankin in her book, *Mind Over Medicine*, the body produces stress hormones when it is in this fight or flight (EHA) mode. These stress hormones are good for getting us out of flight-or-fight situations but only for a very limited time — approximately 90 seconds. However, they become poisonous to the human body when allowed to continue for prolonged periods of time. Doctors continuously warn about the dangers of prolonged anxiety.

The Cure

The confidence that SB and ST paths promote calms the amygdala of the performer and in so doing, reduces the production of stress hormones during the performance. Remember Charl Ann's comment when she arrived to perform her new piece after her initial Stop Bow practice experiment? *"I had no concerns."* No concerns about possible mistakes because there would be none. No concerns about energy depletion because she manufactured it through her SB. No concerns about EHA because her focus drove every note. In other words, she was *confident* in her ability to masterfully perform the music – which she did.

Chapter Seven - Drawing Zone

Drawing Zone: From a Path that Mirrors the SB

Drawing is a solitary discipline. It's not performed before an audience, but it has, nonetheless, a right brain zone where artistic perfection resides. In the *math drawing* sessions, the students are encouraged to use their left brain to get the bones of the drawing into place. Here the left brain is being utilized because the students are not drawing what they *see* but rather what they *hear*. The instructor describes the line in words before he demonstrates it. So the students are listening to words — words that tell them the shape of the line they will be drawing as well as its position on the paper. When the right brain finally comes to the fore is when the students finish the drawing on their own. The perfect, but unfinished picture they have just produced spurs them on to get creative – sometimes with shading or color, but other times with new details they may have seen in their lives that impacted them in some way. This is where the shift to the right-brain zone happens.

Betty Edwards, in her book, *Drawing on the Right Side of the Brain,* has created clever exercises to unlock the door to the right-brain's zone for the fledgling art student. One of these exercises is asking them to copy something the left brain wouldn't be able to decipher, like an upside-down picture. This forces the left brain to retreat and allow the right brain to take over. This exercise helps the brain of the beginning art student to painlessly make the shift from the dominant left brain to the submissive right brain.

Several aspects of Edward's method parallel Stop Bow; in SB practice, no part of the work is more difficult than any other. Edwards, likewise, states that with right-brain drawing, "no subject is harder to draw than any other."

Using the SB path, you *stop* and prepare for each note or move by examining or analyzing and then you position the hands and other body parts in preparation for the perfect execution of that note or move. All this pulls your focus onto that note or move and its perfect execution. Then you perform it perfectly.

Similarly, in right-brain drawing, you first *stop* and look at the scene you will be drawing. But you don't just look at it; you *really* look at it until you see clearly the shape you are going to draw. You examine its position and size in proportion to the spaces you've already outlined before you begin to draw this newest shape. All this preparation pulls your focus into that shape. Then you draw it. An art teacher-friend, Monica Spooner, echoes Betty Edwards when she reminds her students that "Learning how to draw is learning how to see."

In SB practice, the piece of music or dance or *kata* you are practicing is not recognizable until the work is closer to performance level. In right-brain drawing, you don't identify what you are drawing by any term other than the shape you are drawing at that moment. In other words you don't say, "I'm drawing a lake." But rather, "I'm drawing a triangular shape that lines up with the circular shape above it, etc." So, the drawing as a whole is not recognizable until it is close to completion.

These findings of Edwards let us know that a proponent of a more sedentary discipline has discovered a similar path to its artistic zone.

Chapter Eight - The Performance Zone

The "Zone" for the Musician

When the music nears performance level, the muscles gradually begin taking on the major responsibility for the performance, and then the brain's focus now is seemingly from the right hemisphere manifesting itself as a focused *touch*. Obviously, the left brain can't be thinking about more literal things like the names of the notes during the performance because it is way too slow. The right brain however, is super fast and all-encompassing and can handle the speed demanded by the performer. If the left brain shows up at all, it's simply heeding the stress call the EHA is sending out. It will back off as soon as the performer breathes, connects to his focus and allows the right brain to come to the party. If the practices have adhered to the Stop Bow path, the muscles are ready to accept the signals from the right brain. So at that point one could say, "The performer is *in the zone.*"

Whether the brain has a differentiation that is that well delineated remains debatable, but observations from the point of view of the performer tell us that the *zone* the performer goes into during the performance doesn't allow for interference from the left brain. Most of us have heard about an artist who has a photographic memory and can picture each page of the sheet music, so he can in effect "read" his way through the performance. This rare performer is possibly performing from the left brain or may be blending his brain function to incorporate both hemispheres. Most of us don't have the luxury of a photographic memory, however, so we have to depend on our muscles' memory of the music and the focus attached to those muscles to lead us into the zone. The Stop Bow path allows the performer to seamlessly slide into that zone. When he does, he owns the stage.

Of course there are different styles or types of any art form. Performed music tends to fall into two categories. The first is music that is written by a composer. After it is written, the performer must learn and perform the composer's music *note for note*. The audience expects to hear exactly what the composer wrote. Because the notes are predetermined, the performer enters his right-brained zone through his focused energy, passion, and artistry.

Then there is music in which the composer and the artist are *co-creators*. The performer takes the composer's music and plays it as it was written, and then branches off into his own rendition of the work by embellishing the original chord progression with his own musical lines – improvisation. Jazz and folk music often work this way.

Ostensibly, the jazz musician performs using both hemispheres of his brain. He learns his jazz "licks" (memorized lines of music that sound "cool") in a variety of keys, and plays them at the appropriate times during the session. The appropriate times depend on the chords being played by the other musicians. There are copious signals that go on back and forth on the stage to let the musicians know when to start, stop, solo, etc.

It is obvious that left-brain-thinking goes into jazz sessions. But when, however, does the session slip into the right-brain's zone, so it – as the old time jazz players like to say — "starts to *cook?*" It happens when the musicians have their *licks* firmly implanted in body and soul, and the signal and pulse drives the players into the zone. When everybody is in the zone, the session *cooks.*

The Zone for the Martial Arts Competitor

Entering the zone implies a mind-body connection. From time to time, black belts are called upon to sit on panels to judge competitors. It becomes boringly obvious when competitors have zoned out on their *katas*, and are just allowing their muscles to run the show. Occasionally however, I've been present to observe – in the middle of one of these "out of focus" *katas* — a sudden and quite remarkable shift from *no zone* to *zone*. In this situation, it is easy to see the transition from *zone off* to *zone on* because the moves involved are juxtaposed.

Why did this particular shift occur? The most likely answer is that the competitor began his form allowing his muscles to perform it while his brain was asleep or otherwise engaged and then suddenly the form slipped out of his grasp and he was faced with two prospects: walk off the stage in shame, or start faking. He chose the latter.

At this point he is suddenly wide awake and the fight is on. So, because the competitor had suddenly forgotten the *kata*, EHA set in and he began to focus with moves that are driven by the fight scenario alive in his mind. He was now in the zone, and the black belt panel was privileged to witness that shift from zone off to zone on. Unfortunately it's the wrong zone. He didn't win the competition because the black belts judging him knew the form, and that wasn't it. But it was a good show. The zone, in this case was left-brain induced because he had to *think* about every move he was about to make. The ultimate zone should be right-brain driven and stem from focused practices.

Fariborz Azhakh, my *hapkido* master, encouraged his students to compete in tournaments. He knew that competition is a great motivator, and that performance can lead to the *zone* experience. I had been in martial arts for years, but I'd never competed in a tournament. I wasn't interested in getting injured in a *fighting* division. (Before starting *hapkido*, I taught *tae kwan do* for five years and attended most "fight nights" so I was no stranger to the ER for broken, pulled, sprained, dislocated something-or-other, the pain from which always seemed to reach its apex at three a.m. The doctors at the Motion Picture Hospital had begun to recognize me on sight.) Fortunately, there were *kata* divisions available. You couldn't get hurt in a *kata* division unless you hit yourself in the head with your weapon. So, I took Master Fariborz's advice and began competing in some of those for a few years. The experience was wonderful but I didn't begin winning black belt divisions until I started analyzing the movements of the black belt division winners. I noticed that the winners tended to be male. But instead of dwelling on that, I decided to concentrate on what they were doing with their bodies to produce the percussive moves that were winning the divisions. There was no wobbling or jiggling. Every move was decisive, independent, percussive, and powerful. But there was something else. Something that wasn't discernable. I'd seen it in Fariborz's demonstrations, of course, because he was a renowned tournament winner. The eyes hinted at the secret. It finally dawned – it was *focus* but a focus that connected the entire body, and drove every nanosecond of every move. This powerful focus was reflected in the eyes. These winners took the stage immediately and held it until they left it. The energy and passion from that focus radiated from the stage to impact everyone in the house.

But how do you communicate *focus* to a student? Teachers can say "focus" but does that convey what is really happening during that sort of focus? Fariborz would demonstrate and then allow the student a few minutes to absorb it, walk away and let him discover what he thinks he has seen, then he would watch him as he analyzes the move. It was during one of these "walk-aways" that I discovered that the secret ingredient in Fariborz's winning *kata* was that all-encompassing focus. So now that the secret was out, it was time to hop back on the SB path if winning was going to be on the agenda.

I chose to concentrate on a division called Black Belt Showmanship. This division allowed competitors to make up their own *katas,* choreographed to music. It was the most popular division because the music gave it the spark that was missing in other *kata* divisions. And of course the music helped the competitor slide into *the zone.* My son, Robbie, found what he believed to be the best choice for the music, the introduction to "Who Cares Wins" by the heavy metal band, Anthrax. He was right. Every young adult in the stadium knew the music. It evoked an excitement that was instantly zone-producing for the performer.

My weapons of choice were the Chinese double broadswords. I believed I could be successful with these weapons because my hands and forearms were strong and flexible from years of playing piano, because Fariborz was a brilliant teacher, and because I knew the secret to success at anything – the Stop Bow practice path.

Eventually, after much investigation, I developed criteria for the moves I'd create in the form. First the move would have to look and feel right with my body type. That meant I'd have to throw out the dive-roll I'd been doing. Beside the fact that it was hard on my body, it caused every move that followed it to be anticlimactic. Next, it had to fit with the music – and that meant that since the music was percussive, the moves had to be percussive also. Finally, the moves had to show off the strengths of the competitor – and my strength lay in focused spinning of the broadswords.

I knew that the beauty of the Stop Bow method lay not only in its ability to usher in perfection and confidence, but in its ability to *create energy*. When you are nearing the performance, and you're on your 15/15 regimen, if you kick off the *kata's* practice up to speed, you'll burn yourself out early in the regimen. If you begin each practice with the essence of SB, however, you'll *create* energy rather than expend it – energy that will sustain you throughout your practice session.

On tournament day the excitement is palpable. You, the competitor, rise at 4:30 am, or earlier if you have a long commute. All the mundane things like eating and grooming take on new dimensions. Did you consume enough carbohydrates, enough protein? Is your hair style going to add or detract from the performance? Should you polish your toenails? All the things you didn't think about when you were creating the form come to the fore. The last practice before the competition will be SB.

Finally it's time. The judges call your number, you take the stage, bow, approach the panel of judges, introduce yourself and the studio you are representing, present your weapons to the judges who test them for soundness, and hand them back to you. You bow again, take your position, breathe, pray, connect, wait, — and then the music blasts onto the scene, and the *zone begins* – focused, right brain linked to perfect muscle memory, and passion. If the SB practice path is closely adhered to, you can win any division you enter… And I did, seven times. You may ask. "What was so amazing about that?" Answer: If the oldest black belt in the division wins it and if that black belt also happens to be a woman in her fifties competing against every able-bodied black belt in the stadium – man, woman, child — who had the nerve to enter the division, then perhaps the practice method she used should be — at the very least — looked into.

Chapter Nine – Letters of Endorsement

Over the years, Charl Ann's students have voiced what it was about her teaching method that impacted their lives. Not only did it usher in anxiety-controlled perfection in their performances, but it lifted the rest of their lives to a higher level as well. Some of their letters follow.

A Letter from Melodie Arbaban-Ghafouri

My name is Melodie Arbaban-Ghafouri. I have been a violinist for more than thirteen years, eleven of which have been with Mrs. Charl Ann Gastineau. Her method of teaching is very precise and to the point. She meant business from the beginning and that business meant practicing every day with Stop Bow. For the first year-and-a-half we spent every violin lesson refining my technique, and stuck to Book One in the Suzuki series until I was successful. Every lesson was with Stop Bow. Sometimes I left in tears, but I knew the way I was learning would ensure success and that is what I wanted. At the time, I thought Stop Bow lessons were simply torturous, painful and just plain cruel. Every lesson ended with sore fingertips and pure frustration. But as I progressed as a violinist I learned that if I wanted to learn a piece well, the most effective way was by stopping every bow stroke and making sure every note was captured.

My violin lessons forced me to improve my technique to be accurate at every moment. My natural instinct, in the beginning of my violin training, was to rebel against the rules and the strictness of the lessons, but as time went by I learned to appreciate it. I learned to apply every lesson I learned to the situations in my life and to overcome them by being precise and accurate. My violin lessons have gone a long way in teaching me accuracy, precision, and technique. I was home-schooled for most of my schooling and as a result I hadn't faced many academic difficulties. But in eighth grade, when I attended a middle school, the lessons I learned in violin were applied to my daily experience. Facing people and giving speeches weren't a problem, since for years I'd had to perform in recitals and fiddling competitions which compelled me to perform in front of very large audiences. All the practicing has helped me to build a sense of confidence and self-esteem that no one can take from me. I believe the years as a violinist have made me the young lady I am today.

A Letter from Tara Gillaspy

Throughout the many years of taking lessons with Mrs. Gastineau, I have discovered that without the use of the Stop Bow, my performance would have been below my expectations and fairly disappointing. On the other hand, when using Charl Ann's method, I have found my performances have exceeded my expectations.

Stop Bow requires much diligence and focus. In my biweekly lessons, Charl Ann would have me spend the majority of the lesson playing with Stop Bow. After an hour-long lesson, we would usually only get through about eight to sixteen measures of a concerto's first movement. Charl Ann always taught the importance of the quality of practice over the quantity of practice; how you practice is much more essential than the amount of time you put in. The words of Charl Ann – "Ten minutes of practicing with Stop Bow is more beneficial than practicing an hour any other way" – continue to prove true.

I never had a number of hours a day to practice music, but I continually succeeded in playing well at competitions and performances. Looking back, my practicing routine usually consisted of leaving the violin sitting on top of the piano and picking it up multiple times a day for only fifteen to twenty minutes each time. Sometimes it was for only five minutes. It was in those short few minutes, however, that I centered my attention on my bow hold, my fingering, my bow placement, and my strong stop bow. I concentrated on making each note sound 110 percent and nothing less. After many days of practicing this way, I would then spend a small portion of my practicing time gradually speeding up my tempo – this is where I really felt my hard work paying off. Charl Ann was right! It really doesn't take four-to-six hours of mere practice, it takes centered attention on what your hands and fingers are doing – focus, dedication, and clear, concise Stop Bow. Though this may seem tedious, practicing this way makes the most difficult passage of a concerto seem effortless.

A Letter from Tara Brown

I originally learned Charl Ann Gastineau's Stop Bow Method in order to develop my musical ability, but the concepts and practice are applicable to many areas of life.

Practicing music with Stop Bow gives me time to focus on fundamentals such as tone quality and posture. This is a natural extension of the Suzuki Method, which attempts to mimic the way children learn their native language. Using the Suzuki Method, students learn naturally by playing progressively harder pieces rather than learning by playing scales or exercises. In the same way that children learn to speak by making sounds, then words, and then sentences, the Stop Bow Method allows a student to start first with manageable chunks (individual notes) before progressing to musical phrases and then to putting the whole piece together.

Thinking about every note before playing it – how it sounds, what it will feel like, and its relationship to the previous note – gets the piece I am working on into my muscle memory. It also improves basic skills that apply to other pieces of music. I have noticed that it is more helpful to play through a piece one time with everything correct, than to play it ten times with hesitation and mistakes in the difficult passages. If I play a mistake just a couple of times, it starts to be ingrained in my memory and becomes difficult to correct. Playing with mistakes reinforces those mistakes, while playing perfectly reinforces perfection.

The high productivity of Charl Ann's Stop Bow Method is evident during my practice sessions. I feel encouraged when I can see clear progress, which in turn makes practicing more fun. The confidence gained from knowing that the piece is solid, helps my performance, too. Since I practice playing every note with confidence when I practice with Stop Bow, this translates when I perform the piece. Creating the impression of confidence becomes a habit. I still get nervous about public performance, but since the piece is totally ingrained in my muscle memory, with a confident tone and confident body language, it doesn't show.

The Stop Bow strategy has helped me with other tasks as well as with the violin. A few months ago, I bought my first house. The yard was nothing but a fifth of an acre of dirt mixed with asphalt chunks, and getting the yard to look decent on a low budget was quite a daunting prospect. I came up with a plan for the yard and gave myself permission to do a little bit at a time, rather than trying to do the whole thing at once and getting overwhelmed. This deliberate approach of breaking a large task into manageable pieces was first developed by my experience with the Stop Bow Method. It keeps me from initially viewing a task as overwhelming. I figured I could start small by digging up the dirt and planting seeds in just a few square feet every day. I planted five fruit trees over the course of a week. About half the yard is still covered in black plastic, but the rest looks pretty good now.

At a more holistic level, the Stop Bow Method has instilled in me a sense of self-awareness. It's not that I can't do anything spontaneously, but I usually at least consider the implications. I realize that I am constantly making decisions, even if that is a subconscious decision not to consider other choices. The Stop Bow Method has developed in me a mindfulness of all of the small decisions that I make every day. Because this is a habit, it's almost like a computer program running in the background – so automatic that I don't have to use a lot of energy on it. It just happens, and I am sure my life is improved because I am always present in the moment and aware of the consequences of my decisions.

A Letter from Asher Smith

After all my years of playing, I still rely on and use this method, not only when learning new pieces, but also reviewing and going over pieces that need revisiting. It definitely requires an enormous amount of discipline. It is tedious at first, but once you realize the impact that it has on your playing ability and performance, the thought of its being tedious seems to go away.

The Stop Bow Method is not only beneficial for playing and perfecting violin music, it can be applied to other instruments as well. Start off slowly and get everything perfect the first time. Then from there, you gradually speed up. If you start off with a rush, you make yourself much more prone to mistakes and this will hurt your performance level. Just as the Stop Bow Method is used on the violin, it can be applied to picking exercises on the guitar or mandolin, or hitting a snare drum with drumsticks. You don't have to limit yourself to the violin. Apply this method to any instrument you are practicing.

When this method is applied and followed-through correctly, self-esteem can be greatly boosted. When you're practicing, you're usually just by yourself and there is no pressure. But once you go to perform, the pressure can be overwhelming, but you're confident, because you know that you've been practicing correctly for this performance. In most cases you nail it, and do great. Whenever I do well in a performance, it makes me feel better about performing the next time. If you don't have much time to practice, then you'd better make the most of the time you do have. The Stop Bow practice ensures that every note will be perfect then, and later as well.

As I mentioned earlier, reviewing songs and arrangements is vital. After a long layoff, you can get rusty. I have experienced this first-hand. But whenever I come back to pieces that I haven't visited in a while, I go through them and stop the bow before each note is played, focusing on the note and getting every pitch correct. Bottom line: this method works, and should not be taken lightly.

A Letter from Morgan Gillaspy

When I was a violin student of Charl Ann Gastineau's, I was always instructed to use the Stop Bow Method whenever learning a new song and when polishing up an old song for a competition or a recital. Stopping the bow in between every note not only slowed the entire pace of the song down, but gave one time to prepare for the next note. It also provided time to ensure one would be using proper bowing technique and would use plenty of power and control with each bow stroke. Thus, although slow, each note of the song was given equal attention and energy. Nothing was rushed or overlooked. The difficult passages were no longer difficult because the student could go as slowly as needed and simply play one note at a time.

The songs I was diligent in practicing with Stop Bow were the songs that would take me to the top of the competitions. As a child, I learned that patience and consistency paid off, and although it is more fun to play the song fast early on, and easier and less time-consuming, it was never worth it. The songs that were practiced with Stop Bow always sounded ten times better.

Under the high pressure of a fiddling competition, where the competition was stiff, using Stop Bow was a must. I always practiced with Stop Bow before a competition, and if I didn't make time for it, I was sure to regret it afterward. When my name was called to perform, I'd stand up on the stage and my mind would go blank with nervousness. I would be thinking about the people in the audience and about how well the kid before me just played ... but my fingers and my bow arm would be sailing with ease. I would have to remind myself to breathe during the songs. The songs were timed, and I was playing fast, but the notes just flew automatically from within. From the foundation of perfect, slow, consistent Stop Bow practices came the ability to play quickly and flawlessly during those high-intensity performances.

I now teach violin to children and every new song is learned with Stop Bow only. That is the method I learned from Charl Ann, and it is proven to be such a reliable method that I will be forever grateful to her._

A Letter from Dr. Harry Cozen

Charl Ann Gastineau's Stop Bow Method has helped me to learn and perform music. Her principle of slow and accurate practice of a new piece teaches your hands and ears how they should sound and feel. As the correct notes are imprinted on muscle memory and ear memory you develop a more rapid and accurate mastery of the music. This slow and accurate practice takes the place of faster but sloppier playing where mistakes always creep in. Once a mistake is practiced into a piece, it is very hard to unlearn. After you know how the piece should sound and feel it is easy to gradually speed up to the correct tempo. Slow and accurate playing also forces you to engage your mind and mentally concentrate on what you are doing which leads to faster and deeper learning.

Charl Ann Gastineau's Stop Bow Method has helped me to learn and to perform not only on violin, but also on mandolin and piano. I must add that research shows that learning and practicing music is good for the brains of the young and the old. Young people do better in school and old people may be less likely to develop dementia.

A Letter from Rebecca Tseitlin

I began lessons with Charl Ann when I was around nine years old, and she was a formative and formidable influence on my early musical development. I was very enthusiastic about playing violin, and her careful nurturing of my talent really helped me thrive and develop as a young artist. Her success in teaching me was due in a large part to her gentle, yet firm style, which she applied to the Suzuki method and her own Stop Bow Method of learning a new repertoire. I always looked forward to my lessons with Charl Ann and she was a consistently positive motivator who inspired and encouraged me to learn and play with confidence and enjoyment.

The Suzuki method emphasized the importance of learning by ear and learning real repertoire rather than rote exercises, which appealed to me because I was absolutely in love with classical music. The pieces were what I really fell in love with – listening to them, learning them, performing them – I loved the whole process. Charl Ann led me through this process of internalizing pieces by careful insistence on correct intonation, beautiful sound, and accuracy in shifts. The Stop Bow Method was what really carried me from a basic knowledge of a piece to a confident mastery of the piece. I was an impatient student, always asking to move on to the next piece, but learning pieces through the Stop Bow Method forced me to concentrate on each note, one note at a time, to really master the difficulties of a piece before moving on to the next one.

One special performance as Charl Ann's student that I vividly remember was really influenced by the Stop Bow Method of practice. I was learning Mozart's A major concerto for the first time, and I remember practicing diligently with the Stop Bow Method. The technical difficulties and transparency of the piece were a new challenge for me, but through careful, slow practice with this method, the difficulties of fast passagework and high notes lost their intimidation factor completely. Through repetition and careful attention to detail on each and every note, as Charl Ann taught me, I was able to learn the piece to the point where I was confident that it would come out perfectly on stage. I was calm, confident, and excited as I walked out on stage. Everything –all the passagework, the high notes, the clear and transparent opening – all came out perfectly, because of my careful practice habits. I really felt and knew after the experience of learning and successfully performing this piece that I truly could learn and perform anything, even the hardest pieces in the violin repertoire. It was a huge confidence-building experience for me that I never forgot.

The love for music – hearing it, playing it, practicing it, perfecting it, and above all, performing it – has never left me since my days as Charl Ann's student, and I am so grateful to her for pouring herself into my musical development. I have gone on to learn and perform some of the most challenging pieces in the violin repertoire and I know that it has been made possible by the wonderful foundation she laid so carefully for me and so many others.

A Letter from Richard Giacopuzzi

In 1987, my then seven-year-old son, Adam Giacopuzzi, began taking violin lessons from Charl Ann Gastineau. We first saw her students perform at the Ventura County Fair and were impressed by the precision and tone clarity of her group of Suzuki students as they played and performed as a group, and individually. As Adam progressed from ear training to sight reading he went from dutiful student to excited young musician. All this came via Charl Ann's patience, guidance, and her Stop Bow Method of teaching proper timing and intonation. This method had many positive effects on Adam for the following reasons:

It slowed him down. An eight-year-old boy wants to do everything fast and Charl Ann's stop bows made him be deliberate and exacting.

It taught him discipline, both in music timing and intonation, which was something not often seen in young fiddlers.

It taught him to use proper mechanics, which prevents fatigue and prevents bad habits which would later be difficult to correct.

As Adam progressed he drifted away from classical/Suzuki violin and gravitated toward Texas Style (contest) fiddle and bluegrass. In the bluegrass and contest world, young fiddlers are allowed (and even encouraged) to play large, even full sized violins to achieve a "big sound" much to the detriment of intonation, technique and proper mechanics. Charl Ann insisted all her students use violins that were properly sized for them, and working up to a full size only when their hands and arms were able to handle it. Adam progressed from a quarter-size to a full-size violin only when his hands and arms were ready, and to this day, his perfect intonation, drive and mechanics are characteristic of his playing.

When my younger son, Keith, took up mandolin at age eight, Charl Ann became his music teacher, and used the same techniques but adapting them to mandolin. He would practice both classical and bluegrass mandolin under Charl Ann's tutelage, focusing on proper timing and pick direction. You could say "pick direction" is the mandolin's version of stop bows. Under her guidance and direction Keith was named Discovery Artist for the New West Symphony in the year 2000. With that orchestra, he played Vivaldi's Mandolin Concerto as the soloist. But watching him memorize and practice that musical piece was a testament to Charl Ann and her teaching methods.

Charl Ann has left a great musical legacy with my family and today both boys (now men) still are involved in music both as hobbies and professionally. I will always be grateful for the knowledge, time, patience, and love she has shown us over the years.

A Note from Michael Leppert

I wish I had had the Stop Bow Method to use in my singing and guitar work. Over time, I developed so much performance anxiety that I quit playing in public. I think if I had had the SB approach to dealing with the EHA (extreme high anxiety), I might have found it enjoyable enough to continue. I continued writing songs and still hope to place some of them with publishers or recording artists, but there is no anxiety in the writing department!

Conclusion

When all is said and done, did you give each note or move its due diligence. Whether one agrees or not with the *why* of the Stop Bow path, the fact remains that it works for the vast majority of students. If you still have doubts, I challenge you to try it. You will be amazed.

There will always be EHA moments in performances, but the SB practice path will aid you in *using* them to benefit the performance.

There will always be students that keep doing the same things over and over expecting a different result, and they will always be amazed when they find that the SB practice path stops this cycle.

There will always be new scientific breakthroughs that will yield more information about the brain, muscles, etc. that will cause scientists to readjust their interpretations of previously collected data. But regardless of which part of the brain is dominant for an individual or what it takes for an individual to succeed, it's an individual pursuit and an individual path to achieving one's goals. If whatever you're doing isn't working, change the path, and make sure that new path yields perfect results at every step. In performance, w*e learn in spite of our mistakes, not because of them.* Don't enter the initial practice or any practice with the fear of being blindsided. Enter it knowing perfection is at hand.

It's your choice. You can choose to make mistakes or not. Relax and *let* your muscles and brain learn by the focused, connected, perfect performing of each note or move. *Play every note or execute every move as if you mean it.* If you're diligent, eventually your brain will come to *believe* that the music or move is present in your muscles, just waiting for your focused signal to produce it.

Charl Ann, in another of her innovative moments mused: "I've often wondered if I could become a world-class golfer using the SB practice path. For several months, I'd practice putting by beginning each practice with the focused perfect swing that I'd been taught by my golf professional. That perfect swing would include reading the green so the club face could be squared up with the hole, distance control, the grip, the feet, knees, shoulders, weight shift, and everything else that pertains to the swing. However, I'd set up a situation where I couldn't fail like placing the ball on the practice-green but only one inch from the hole. I'd focus on the appropriate spot on the ball and in very slow motion, staying aware of every aspect and nanosecond of the swing and never taking my eyes from that spot on the ball, swing toward that spot. I'd never make a mistake. Every stroke would be perfect. A few days later, I'd move the ball two inches from the hole and start again. A few days after that it would be three inches. Eventually, I'd measure the distance from the hole in feet instead of inches. My confidence would never waver because there would never be the contemplation of mistakes. I'd make sure there were no mistakes to cloud my confidence.

"Then I'd get off the green and begin each chipping practice with the focused perfect form I'd learned from my instructor, but with the ball only one foot from the green. Then again I'd line up my club face with the hole, focus on the appropriate spot on the ball, slowly swing toward that spot staying aware of every tiny increment of the swing, and chip the ball with a short slow stroke onto the green toward the hole. I'd do this for several days before moving the ball two feet from the green and repeating the process, then days later three feet, then four, etc… Every ball would land on the green toward the hole. That is perfection.

"Finally I'd move to the tee, learn the perfect form from my instructor, and then use it to slowly make a quarter-swing toward the ball so slowly that it was impossible to miss. Every tiny increment of the swing would be perfect. After days of this, the quarter-swing would increase to a half-swing, but still focused and slow. Eventually the half-swing would become a whole-swing, but still focused and so slow it would remain perfect. Finally the groove of the swing would be established well enough for the speed of the swing to increase.

She is saying that *practice makes perfect if every step in the practice is perfect in its focus, form, and execution. Always expect a perfect result, and never be surprised when it occurs. Relax. Enjoy the journey.*

To wrap up:
Do we focus on every word we say before we say it? Perhaps gifted

speakers do.

Do we focus on every note we sing before we sing it? Perhaps gifted singers do.

Do we focus on every note we play before we play it? Perhaps gifted musicians do.

Do we focus on every step we take before we take it? Perhaps gifted dancers do.

Do we focus on every stroke we make before we make it? Perhaps gifted golfers do.

It is my hope that by reading this book you will discover the joy and satisfaction that can come from applying this strategy to whatever activity is your passion, and with it you will become the best you can be. And, if you are a teacher, you will learn how to unleash the beautiful power of the Stop Bow practice path in both your students, and yourself.

Enjoy!

Epilogue

I want to always be able to motivate and inspire my students as they have inspired me.
I used to have good and bad teaching days, now they are all good.

Charl Ann Gastineau

Anxiety-free perfection in your practice will lead to anxiety-controlled perfection in your performance.

Mary Smale

Websites:

Some of the websites where Charl Ann's former students can be heard are:
www.laurendonahuemusic.com
www.mariachicamarillo.com

Or you may Google the following former students to hear some of their performances:
Keith Giacopuzzi (Mandolin)
Adam Giacopuzzi (Fiddle)
Ashley Broder (Fiddle and Mandolin)

Bibliography

Cabane, Olivia Fox, *The Charisma Myth*, 2013, Portfolio Penguin, New York, New York

Doman, Glen, Developer of the *Better Baby Course*

Edwards, Betty, *Drawing on the Right Side of the Brain*, 1979, J.P. Tarcher, Inc., Los Angeles

Leaf, Dr. Caroline, *Who Switched Off My Brain?*, 2009, Improv Ltd., Phoenix, Arizona

Proceedings of the National Academy of Sciences

Rankin, Lissa, M.D., *Mind Over Medicine*, 2013, Hay House, Carlsbad, California

Sandor, Gyorgy, *On Piano Playing Motion, Sound and Expression,* 1995, Simon & Schuster Macmillan, Australia

Science News (an online publication)

Starr, William and Constance, *To Learn with Love*, 1983, Kingston Ellis Press, Knoxville, Tennessee

Suzuki, Shinichi, *The Suzuki Concept*, 1973, Diablo Press, Inc., Berkeley, California

Acknowledgements:

My deepest thanks to Charl Ann Gastineau, Master Fariborz Azhakh, Master Dennis Ishikawa, Nancy Chaubell, Marian Weiser, Bob Renolds, Ruth Friedman, Morgan Haight, Lauren Rosales, Lennon Leppert, Michael Leppert, Robert Ramirez, David Christian Smale, Vivian Coyle, Rick Barry, and all the masters, teachers, parents and students for their assistance and words of encouragement.

Index

A

About Teaching **9**
About the Book **8**
About the Title **8**
About Us. **12**
Acknowledgements: **124**
   Bob Renolds 124
   Charl Ann Gastineau. 124
   David Christian Smale. 124
   Lauren Rosales 124
   Lennon Leppert 124
   Marian Weiser. 124
   Master Dennis Ishikawa 124
   Master Fariborz Azhakh 124
   Michael Leppert 124
   Morgan Haight 124
   Nancy Chaubell 124
   Rick Barry 124
   Robert Ramirez. 124
   Ruth Friedman 124
   Vivian Coyle 124
A Letter from Eva Masarang **13**
A Note To My Sister, Mary Smale **9**

B

Bibliography. **123**
   Cabane, Olivia Fox. 123
   Edwards, Betty 123
   Leaf, Dr. Caroline. 123
   Proceedings of the National Academy of Sciences 123
   Rankin, Lissa, M.D. 123
   Sandor, Gyorgy. 123
   Science News. 123
   Starr, William and Constance. 123
   Suzuki, Shinichi 123

C

Chapter 1 – The Violin **14**
   Adjusting the Mandolin 40
   A Favorite Idea from Another Teacher. 17

Amount of Time Using SB 37
An Interesting Aside 34
Automatic Playing 39
Back Stage – Getting Ready to Go On. 42
Back to Mary's Narrative.. 32
Before the Performance... 32
Charl Ann's Narrative and Her Steps for a Stop Bow Practice............. 27
Erosion in the Digital Age... 15
Even Practice: 38
Evolution of the Program: Who Is the Teacher Here?..................... 16
Fiddling 18
Fixing a Mistake 39
How the Fiddling Began 19
In One Day? 42
In Summary 36
Keeping the Interest.. 16
Lesson One's Practice Steps... 30
Lesson Three 31
Lesson Two 31
Mandolin Success Stories 21
Matching the Size of the Violin to the Student. 40
Memorizing the Music 41
Mistake in SB Practice... 39
Offering Stop Bow to the Rest of the Students......................... 31
Other Avenues to Success: All Charl Ann's Violin Students Play Mandolin ... 20
Parent Participation 40
Performance Pieces 41
Pitch (Intonation).. 37
Plateaus May Disappear with SB 29
Playing by Ear... 38
Q & A (Charl Ann answers the most frequently asked SB questions)....... 37
Rhythm 38
SB and Relaxation.. 40
Seasoning Time 29
Subsequent SB Practice Sessions 29
Tell Me Again 43
The First Experience Using Stop Bow with a Student.................... 30
The Lament 23
The Nine Potential Mistakes in Violin Technique....................... 24
The Origin of the Stop Bow Method 25
The Secret's Out 33
The Suzuki Method 14
The Ten Fundamental Elements of Aggravation 24
The Workshops: The Magic.. 21
Viewing a SB Success... 35

When to Start/Stop SB?... 42
When to Use SB Practice.. 39
Why Only Once a Day?... 41

Chapter 2 – Piano **44**
A New Language 46
Another Contributing Factor (Lack of Time) 54
A Shameful Beginning... 44
Childhood Ability 61
Consistent Discipline.. 51
Ethel Bartlett Robertson's Singing Tone Method: Stop Bow for the Piano..... 44
Experiment with ST/SB Practice: Pick a Piece........................ 50
Final Analysis 59
Hands-Separate Practice... 50
How did Ethel Know it Wasn't ST? 54
Ideas on Focus from Other Performers.............................. 55
Patterns 65
Practice Makes Perfect if the Practice Was Perfect 57
Putting the Hands Together 50
Q. & A. (Answers to the most frequently asked questions)............. 60
Resurrecting Old Music.. 60
Revisiting the Piano... 56
Scales and Arpeggios.. 64
Sight Reading and Performance Pieces............................... 65
Steps for the ST/SB/Suzuki Practice Session 47
ST/SB and the Artist.. 63
The Doorbell Experiment 46
The Goal 62
The Recital's Job 59
The Similarities and Differences in ST and SB....................... 47
The Singing Tone Touch – Total Focus 45
This Approach.. 59
Why?.. 53

Chapter 3 – Martial Arts **66**
15/15 Countdown to Performance Rule 76
A Black Belt's Perspective on a White Belt Kata...................... 69
Aikido 75
But Which Style Will Preclude the Need for the Other 78
Depletion of Energy... 76
Do We Learn From Our Mistakes? 68
Imaginary Audience... 77
In Summary 76
Making the Connections... 72
More Good News 75
Our Family's Introduction to Martial Arts: Tang Soo Do 66
Pointers from the Dancer 73

Regarding Bullies 78
SB and Hard Style vs. Soft Style 77
Stop Bow for Martial Arts: A Focused Mind-Muscle Connection 66
Tae Kwan Do. 66
The Look 69
The Low Block 70
Think Camera. 74
Using the Stop Bow Path. 69

Chapter 4 – Teaching: Mathematics and Drawing **80**
Evolution of the Stop Bow Path for Math 80
In Summary 88
Marketing the Mathematics to Students through Drawing 83
Stop Bow for TV Math Show Performances. 84
Taking a Lesson from Video Game Creators 82
That's Fine for My Performance, But Was I Forgetting the Students?. 87

Chapter 5 – Science Opinions **90**
Extreme High Anxiety (EHA) 93
Good News Bad News. 91
The Brain's Role in Performance 92

Chapter 6 – Extreme High Anxiety (EHA) **96**
Can a Performer Use the Time-Slowed Element His EHA Produces to His Advantage? . 102
Does EHA Drive Time?. 99
From the Victim's Point of View. 96
Frozen With Fear (EHA). 99
How Healthy is EHA? 103
The Cure 103

Chapter 7 – Drawing Zone. **104**
Drawing Zone: From a Path that Mirrors the SB. 104

Chapter 8 - The Performance Zone. **106**
The Zone for the Martial Arts Competitor. 107
The Zone for the Musician 106

Chapter 9 – Letters of Endorsement **110**
A Letter from Asher Smith 113
A Letter from Dr. Harry Cozen 115
A Letter from Melodie Arbaban-Ghafouri. 110
A Letter from Morgan Gillaspy 114
A Letter from Rebecca Tseitlin. 115
A Letter from Richard Giacopuzzi. 116
A Letter from Tara Brown. 111
A Letter from Tara Gillaspy 111
A Note from Michael Leppert 117

Conclusion. **118**

E

Epilogue **121**

Charl Ann Gastineau 121
Mary Smale 121

I

Introduction **10**

W

Websites **122**
www.laurendonahuemusic.com 122
www.mariachicamarillo.com 122